Concise Visual Basic 6.0 Course

Visual Basic for Beginners

By

Souleiman Valiev

This book is a work of non-fiction. Names and places have been changed to protect the privacy of all individuals. The events and situations are true.

ISBN: 1-4107-6428-1 (e-book)
ISBN: 1-4107-6429-X (Paperback)

This book is printed on acid free paper.

1st Books - rev. 08/14/03

About the Book

This book will teach you fundamental skills, topics and programming techniques for Microsoft® Visual Basic® 6.0. It is an intensive programming course for beginners. Each lesson covers one or more major programming topics, which are related to a corresponding programming task, and assigns a homework project. This approach will allow you to build a strong relationship between theoretical concepts and their practical implementation in a project. More importantly, the approach makes the course unique: it will allow you to jumpstart on a short but intensive training track to develop hands-on programming skills. Structurally, each lesson consists of three parts. Part A reminds you to create, debug and test your homework project described in the previous lesson. Part B introduces a programming topic and gives practical examples. Part C gives a detailed explanation of and systematic instructions for creating your homework project, as well as all the necessary code for the project.

On completing the course you will be able to develop, debug and test advanced Windows® programs using Microsoft® Visual Basic® 6.0 as a programming language.

Summary of Contents

Lesson 1: Introduction to Programming

Lesson 2: How to Use the Visual Basic® Programming Tools

Lesson 3: The Form Object's Properties, Methods and Events

Lesson 4: How to Program the Visual Basic® Controls

Lesson 5: Understanding the Variables and Data Types

Lesson 6: How to Create Functions and Subroutines

Lesson 7: Using the ADO Objects to Retrieve Data

Lesson 8: Using Class Modules and Creating Objects

Lesson 9: Binding COM Servers to Client Applications

Lesson 10: Application Debugging

Lesson 11: Application Error Handling

Lesson 12: How to Create Menus and Open Files

Lesson 13: How to Use Sub Main and the Login Form

Lesson 14: How to Create a Setup Program

The information in this book is sold without warranty, either express or implied. Neither the author, Souleiman Valiev, nor the publisher or distributors will be held liable for any damages caused or alleged to be caused either directly or indirectly by this book.

Table of Contents

Lesson 1 Introduction to Programming **3**

Part A A Visual Basic® Program from a User's Perspective 7

    1. Presentation of a Program's Operation Tools................ 7

    2. What is a Program's Functionality? 8

    3. Understanding a Program's Output and Input 9

    4. What is an Interactive Program?................................... 11

Part B: Analysis of a Demonstration Program **13**

    1. The Program's User Interface...................................... 13

    2. The Program's Functionality 15

Part C: A Program from a Programmer's Perspective **19**

    1. The Program in Design Mode....................................... 19

    2. How the Program's Operation Tools are Created?...... 22

    3. Understanding the Program's Code.............................. 24

Lesson 2 How to Use the Visual Basic® Programming Tools...... 33

Part A Understanding the Visual Basic® Development Tools
.... 37

1. Using Visual Basic® to Develop Programs................. 37

   a) The User Interface Design 38

   b) Writing Code 39

2. Opening the VB Development Program for the First
Time 40

3. Practice at Using Visual Basic to Create a New Project
.... 44

4. The Visual Basic® Development Program Operation
Tools 47

   a) Using the Menu Bar and the Toolbar..................... 48

   b) The Menu Bar... 49

   c) The Toolbar... 51

   d) The Context Menu 51

5. The Visual Basic Development Program Components 53

   a) The Project Explorer 53

   b) The Toolbox 55

   c) The Form Designer and the Toolbox 56

d) The Properties Window 58

e) The Code Editor 59

Part B How to Create a Simple VB Program 63

1. Project Development Plan 63

2. Project Development Plan in Detail 64

a) Step 1. Create and Save a New Standard EXE
Project 64

b) Step 2. Add Controls and Set their Properties 65

c) Step 3. Write Code 67

d) Step 4. Save your Work 68

e) Step 5. Run the Program 68

Part C.Homework Assignment Project 69

1. Create and Save Project 1: *MyFirst* 69

2. Add Controls and Set their Properties 70

a) Open the Form Designer 70

b) Open the Toolbox 71

c) Set the Properties of Objects 72

3. Write the Application Code 73

a) Open the Code Editor 73

b) Write the Click Event Procedures 74

4. Save Your Work 75

5. Run and Test the Application 76

a) Run the Application 76

b) Test the Show and the Clear Buttons 77

Lesson 3 The Form Object's Properties, Methods and Events 81

Part A. Create Your Homework Project 85

1. Project Development, Debugging and Testing Practice
.... 85

**Part B.The Visual Basic® Form Object's Properties,
Methods and Events.. 87**

1. The Visual Basic Form Control 88

2. Setting the Form's Properties at Design and Run Time
.... 89

a) Design Time and Runtime Concepts 89

b) Practice the Design Time Method 91

c) Practice the Runtime Method 91

d) Practice Setting the CommandButton's Properties 93

3. The Form Load Event 94

4. The Unload Method 95

Part C.Homework Assignment Project 97

1. Create and Save Project 2: *FormProperties* 97

2. Add Controls and Set their Properties 98

a) Add Controls... 98

b) Set the Properties of Objects 99

3. Write the Application Code 101

4. Save Your Work 104

5. Run and Test the Application 104

Lesson 4 How to Program the Visual Basic® Controls.......... 109

Part A. Create Your Homework Project........................... 113

1. Project Development, Debugging and Testing Practice
.... 113

Part B.How to Program the VB Controls........................... 115

1. Understanding the VB Controls................................ 115

2. How to Read or Write the Object's Property............. 117

a) Reading the Object's Property 117

b) Setting the Object's Property 119

c) What is the Read-Only Property? 120

d) The Object's Default Property 121

3. Programming the TextBox Control 122

4. Programming the CommandButton 123

a) The CommandButton's Properties 123

b) The CommandButton's Events 124

5. How to Program the Label Control 125

6. Programming the ComboBox 127

Part C. Homework Assignment Project 131

1. Create and Save Project 3: *UsingControls* 131

2. Add Controls and Set their Properties 132

3. Write the Application Code 134

4. Save Your Work 136

5. Run and Test the Application 136

Lesson 5 Understanding Variables and Data Types.............. 141

Part A.Create Your Homework Project............................. 145

1. Project Development, Debugging and Testing Practice
.... 145

Part B.Understanding Variables and Data Types 147

1. What is a Variable?... 147

2. Understanding Data Types 150

3. Practice Creating Variables 152

4. Practice Assigning Values to Variables..................... 154

5. Understanding the Null, Empty and Zero-Length String
.... 155

6. Understanding the Variable Scope 161

Part C.Homework Assignment Project 165

1. Create and Save Project 4: *UsingDataTypes* 165

2. Add Controls and Set their Properties 166

3. Write the Application Code 169

4. Save Your Work 172

5. Run and Test the Application 172

Lesson 6 How to Create Functions and Subroutines.............. **177**

Part A.Create Your Homework Project **181**

1. Project Development, Debugging and Testing Practice
.... 181

Part B.How to Create Functions and Subroutines **183**

1. Code Modularization Concept 183

2. Procedures are not Created Equal 185

3. Procedures and Variables.. 186

4. What is a Subroutine Procedure?.............................. 186

5. A Procedure Scope Concept 187

6. How to Use Functions and Subroutines..................... 188

    a) Practice Creating Subs 189

    b) How to Use the Procedure Argument List........... 190

    c) Passing Procedure Parameters ByVal and ByRef 192

    d) How to Call a Procedure....................................... 195

    c) Practice Creating Functions 197

7. Procedures and Algorithms....................................... 199

    a) Event Procedures and Independent Procedures ... 199

Part C. Homework Assignment Project 207

    1. Create and Save Project 5: *CreatingProcedures* 207

    2. Add Controls and Set their Properties 208

    3. Write the Application Code 210

    4. Save Your Work 215

    5. Run and Test the Application 215

Lesson 7 Using the ADO to Retrieve Data.............................. 219

Part A. Create Your Homework Project............................. 223

    1. Project Development, Debugging and Testing Practice
    223

Part B. Using the ADO to Retrieve Data 225

    1. Understanding the SQL Statements........................... 225

    2. How to Program the ADO Connection Object 228

        a) Step 1: Reference the ADO library..................... 229

        b) Step 2: Declare a Connection Object Variable.... 229

        c) Step 3: Create a Connection Object..................... 230

        d) Step 4: Set the Connection Object's Properties... 230

e) Step 5: Open Connection 231

3. How to Create and Use the ADO Recordset Object .. 232

   a) Step 1: Declare a Recordset Object Variable 233

   b) Step 2: Create the Recordset Object 233

   c) Step 3: Build a SQL Query 233

   d) Step 4: Open the Recordset 234

4. How to Display the ADO Recordset Data in a Grid
Control 235

   a) How to Read a Single Record 235

   b) How to Display Multiple Records 237

5. How to Use the *If* Statement 238

Part C. Homework Assignment Project 241

1. Create and Save Project 6: *UsingADOObjects* 241

2. Add Controls and Set their Properties 242

3. Write the Application Code 244

4. Save Your Work 260

5. Run and Test the Application 261

Lesson 8 Using Class Modules and Creating Objects 267

Part A.Create Your Homework Project 271

1. Project Development, Debugging and Testing Practice
.... 271

Part B.Using Class Modules and Creating Objects 273

1. Applications and Components Tandem 273

2. Understanding Objects and Classes 274

   a) Advantages of Using Objects 275

3. The Object's Methods, Properties and Events 277

   a) How to Create the Object's Methods 278

   b) How to Create the Object's Properties 279

   i) Practice Using the Procedural Method 280

   ii) Practice Using the Declarative Method 283

   c) How to Create the Object's Events 284

4. How to View the Object in the Object Browser 286

5. A COM DLL and Classes 288

6. How to Create a COM DLL 290

Part C.Homework Assignment Project 293

1. Create and Save Project 7: *ObjectsAndClasses* 293

2. Add Controls and Set their Properties 295

3. Add Three Class Modules to the Project 297

4. Write the Application Code 299

    a) Write Code in the Event Procedures 300

    b) Write Procedures and Functions 304

Lesson 9 Binding COM Servers to Client Applications 315

Part A.Create Your Homework Project 319

1. Project Development, Debugging and Testing Practice
.... 319

Part B.Binding COM Servers to Client Applications 321

1. Understanding Object Binding 321

2. Two Methods of Object Binding 323

    a) Early Binding 323

    b) Late Binding 324

3. Practice Object Binding Techniques 325

Part C.Homework Assignment Project 331

1. Complete Project 7: *ObjectsAndClasses* 331

2. Write Code in Each Class Module............................ 332

   a) Write the following code in the cCamera class
   module. 332

   b) Write the following code in the cCamcorder class
   module. 337

   c) Write the following code in the cConnector class
   module. 342

   d) View your Objects in the Object Browser........... 346

3. Run and Test the Application 348

   a) Foolproof Testing 348

   b) Application Functionality Testing....................... 350

   c) Bugs Known to Dwell in this Application........... 352

   d) The Delete Button Bug...................................... 353

   e) The Edit Button Bug.. 353

   f) How to Catch the Bugs 353

Lesson 10 Application Debugging 357

Part A. Create Your Homework Project............... 361

1. Project Development, Debugging and Testing Practice 361

    a) Complete Project 7 361

    b) Application Bugs 362

    c) Test the Application 362

Part B.Application Debugging 363

    1. Design Time and Runtime Errors 363

        a) Design Time Errors 363

        b) Runtime Errors 364

    2. How to Use Breakpoints 367

    3. Practice Using Breakpoints 368

        a) Debug the AddProduct procedure 368

        b) How to Use the Immediate Window 369

Part C.Homework Assignment Project 373

    1 Create and Save Project 8: *ObjectsAndClassesDG* 374

    2. Debug the Application 375

        a) Analysis of the Delete Button Bug 375

        b) The Delete Button Bug Fix 380

        c) Analysis of the Edit Button Bug 382

d) The Edit Button Bug Fix 382

3. Write the Application Code 383

4. Run and Test the Application 385

Lesson 11 Application Error Handling.................................. 389

Part A. Create Your Homework Project 393

1. Project Development, Debugging and Testing Practice 393

Part B.Application Runtime Error Handling 395

1. Error Handling 395

2. Design Time Errors.. 397

3. Internal Logical Errors... 400

a) Logical Errors 401

b) Programming Errors 402

4. How to Write Error Handlers 404

Part C. Homework Assignment Project 411

1. Create and Save Project 9: ObjectsAndClassesEH ... 411

2. Write Error Handling Code 412

3. Run and Test the Application 416

Lesson 12 How to Create Menus and Open Files................... 421

Part A. Create Your Homework Project 425

1. Project Development, Debugging and Testing Practice
.... 425

Part B.How to Create Menus and Open Files 427

1. Creating Menus... 427

2. How to Programmatically Open Files........................ 432

   a) File Open Methods... 433

   b) How to Write a File Open Statement................... 435

3. How to Programmatically Read from a File 437

5. File Open Error Handling 440

   a) File not Found Runtime Error.............................. 441

   b) End of File (EOF) Error....................................... 446

2. Redesign the frmMenus Form 451

   a) Remove TextBoxes, Labels and CommandButtons.
   451

   b) Create Menus... 451

3. Add Controls and Set their Properties 454

4. Write the Application Code. 456

5. Write the AddProduct Sub.. 459

5. Run and Test the Application 475

Lesson 13 How to Use the Sub Main and a Login Form 479

Part A. Create Your Homework Project............................ 483

1. Project Development, Debugging and Testing Practice
.... 483

Part B.How to Use the Sub Main and a Login Form 485

1. The Sub Main as a Program Startup Object 485

2. How to Create a Login Form 487

3. How to Program the MsgBox Function..................... 488

   a) The MsgBox Function Arguments 489

   b) How to Use the MsgBox() Function's Return Value
   495

4. How to Compile an Application 498

Part C. Homework Assignment Project 501

1. Create and Save Project 11: LoginProject................. 502

2. Add Controls and Set their Properties 504

3. Write the Application Code 506

    a) Write the Sub Main procedure 507

    b) Write code in the frmLogin form 507

4. Run and Test the Application 515

5. Compile your Application... 516

6. Extra Credit Tasks... 517

Lesson 14 How to Create a Setup Program............................ 521

Part A. Create Your Homework Project 525

1. Create Project 11 525

2. Project 11 Bug Description 525

3. Project 11 Bug Fix 526

4. Project 11 Extra Credit Task 530

Part C. How to Create an Installation Program 533

1. What is a Setup Program?.. 533

2. How a Program is Installed? 534

    a) Granting a Permanent Resident Status................. 534

   b) Copying Files and Registering Components 535

   3. How does a Setup Program Work? 536

   4. How to Create an Installation Program 537

   5. How to Uninstall a Program 538

Part D. Homework Assignment Project 541

   1. Create *Project12* Folder 542

   2. Compile the Application 543

   3. Create the Application Setup Program 543

   4. Run the Setup Program on your Computer 558

   5. Run and Test the Installed Program 559

Lesson 1

Lesson 1

Introduction to Programming

In this Lesson:

Y ou will learn how a computer program works and how it is designed. You will be introduced to basic computer programming concepts. To illustrate these concepts we will analyze a special demonstration program from a user's perspective and then look at the same program from a programmer's perspective.

Contents of Lesson 1

Part A: A Visual Basic® Program from a User's Perspective

1. Presentation of a Program's Operation Tools

2. What is a Program's Functionality?

3. Understanding a Program's Output and Input

4. What is an Interactive Program?

Part B: Analysis of a Demonstration Program

1. The Program's User Interface

2. The Program's Functionality

Part C: A Program from a Programmer's Perspective

1. The Program in Design Mode

2. How the Program's Operation Tools are Created?

3. Understanding the Program's Code

4. Learn Programming Terms

A Visual Basic® Program from a User's Perspective

1. Presentation of a Program's Operation Tools

A program can be used to complete actions. A user can initiate those actions if a program provides some operation tools. Most windows programs use various visual images to build a program's virtual operation tools. Let us look at how this is realized in a program created using Visual Basic as the programming language.

When the user starts a windows-based program, the first thing it does is show a window. A window is actually a visual image that is made up of certain visual elements that represent various program functionality tools. When a programmer designs this visual image, he or she tries to make sure that it is easily understood, intuitive, and able to present its functionality both explicitly and implicitly. For instance, when a programmer places a label "First Name:" before a text box he explicitly declares the function of that text box in the program. When he uses a book icon as a hyperlink to a document that contains some help topics, he implies that this is a help tool. Thus, various visual elements, such as push buttons, text boxes and check boxes, make up a program's virtual operation tools.

2. What is a Program's Functionality?

A program is designed with a certain user or a group of users in mind; in other words, a program must be useful to a certain category of users and should be able to perform certain actions. For example, the Notepad program is used to create, edit, archive or print text files. From this point of view, any program has two major aspects. The first aspect is what functionality a program can provide and the second aspect is how a program works. A program's functionality is what the program can do and what the user expects from it. For example, a program can create a report, calculate taxes or create a file. As for the program's work, it can be generally described by three major operations: data input, data processing and data output. Note the term data in this context means any information that a program can receive, process and present to the user. Once any information is entered into a program, it qualifies as data.

3. Understanding a Program's Output and Input

The process of receiving information may generally be called data input while the process of directing information to the consumer may be called data output. In most cases, a program's output is a presentation of certain information to a user. The selection of such information may be preset by the program or it may be carried out dynamically based on the criteria provided by the user when the program is running.

The information may be presented in various forms: textual, graphical, audio and visual. The user's information request is an example of a program's input and may be used as the selection criteria. The information brought back and displayed by the program is the program output. Of course, there are programs that may run in unattended mode. In those cases the program has no user interaction and may interact with other programs while the input and the output may be provided by various automatic processes.

Figure 1.1 A Program's Interaction with a User.

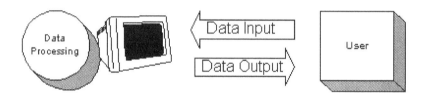

In Figure 1.1, you can see a diagram that illustrates the concept of user interaction with a program. In most real-world situations, both data input and data output may have many methods and forms. For example, data input may come from a floppy disk or from a file on the hard drive and data output may be directed to a printer or to an audio device.

4. What is an Interactive Program?

If a program is able to input, output and process information in response to certain user actions then it is a user interactive program. A user interaction with the program is an example of a human-machine communication dialog. Thus, a program that allows any type of information exchange process is an interactive program. Using Visual Basic as a programming language, you can create both user interactive programs and programs that run in an unattended mode.

Analysis of a Demonstration Program

1. The Program's User Interface

Let's recap: a program may have one or more windows that make up a program's combined visual image. A window or a set of windows created and used in a program is called the program's user interface. A window is typically a visual image drawn on the computer screen. Thus, we often use another term to refer to this image: a graphical user interface, GUI. For the purposes of this discussion, let's divide the user interface into three functional areas: the input area, the output area and the operation tools area. Now that we are armed with a few computer guru terms, we are ready to look at a demonstration program that illustrates all these concepts. We have developed a relatively simple application to present a typical program

created with Visual Basic as a programming language. We called it

the Check Typing Rate program. The program's mission is obvious

from its name.

Figure 1.2 The Check Typing Rate Program's User Interface.

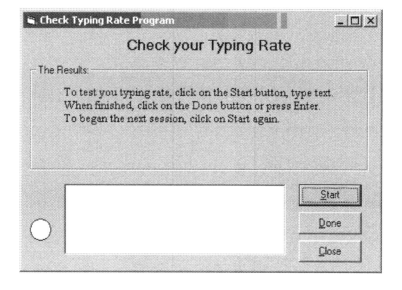

In Figure 1.2, you can see the program's user interface, in

which the upper part is used to dynamically display the program's

output. In this case, the program's output is a calculation of a user's typing rate and some statistics. The lower part of the user interface is used to accept the program's input. In our case, the input is the text typed by the user in a large TextBox. The third functional area of the program is a set of controls that are used to operate the program. All these controls are presented by the so-called push buttons named Start, Done and Close.

2. The Program's Functionality

Here's a short description of the program's functionality: When the program opens it automatically displays instructions for using it. The user is expected to click on the Start button, type any text and when finished click on the Done button or press the Enter key. The results of the typing rate calculation and typing statistics are displayed in the program's output area. In Figure 1.3, you can see the program's user interface after the Start button is clicked.

Figure 1.3. The program's screen after the Start button is clicked.

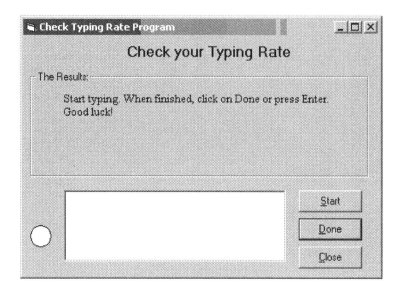

When the Start button is clicked, the program displays an instructional message and the cursor is moved into the text box. The user may now type and then click on the Done button or press the Enter key.

Figure 1.4 The program displays the results.

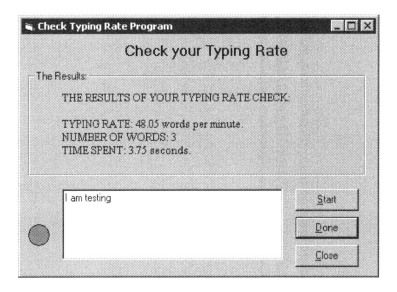

Figure 1.4, shows the user interface that displays the results of the typing test after the user has finished typing and clicked on the Done button. In this test I typed "I am testing" and pressed the Enter key. The program processed the input information by applying the code that was written in it and then presented the output information in the upper part of the user interface.

A Program from a Programmer's Perspective

1. The Program in Design Mode

Now let's look at the same program from a computer programmer's perspective. This will be a virtual journey from the program's user interface to the program's source code, a Visual Basic developer's domain. We will now open the Check Typing Rate program in the Visual Basic development program, which is known as the Visual Basic Integrated Development Environment (IDE). Note in our further discussions, we may use the abbreviation VB IDE.

Figure 1.5 The Check Typing Rate program in the initial design stage.

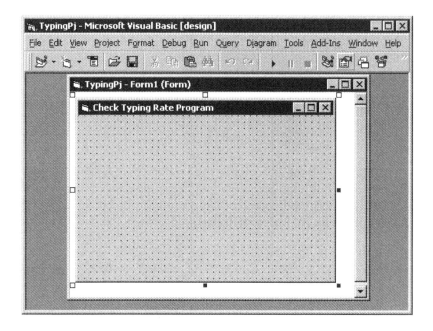

In Figure 1.5, you can see the Check Typing Rate project opened in the VB IDE. This is how the Check Typing Rate project looked at the initial design stage. In this project, we have used a VB form to create the user interface. The form is empty at this point.

Figure 1.6 The Check Typing Rate Program in Design Mode.

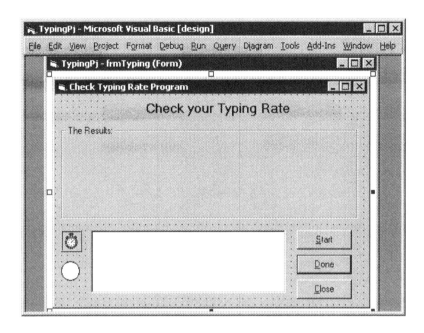

In Figure 1.6, you can see the Check Typing Rate program when all the visual images that make up the program's user interface are in place. At this stage the user interface design is complete.

2. How the Program's Operation Tools are Created?

Most programs created for windows operating systems show a certain visual image called a window. A typical program may use one or more such windows. In this demonstration program, there is only one window, which we have created using the VB Form control. In Figure 1.6, you can see this form in design mode. All visual elements on this form are generated by the VB Controls. In this program, the following VB controls are used: a label, a TextBox, a CommandButton, a shape and a frame.

A Click Event Mechanism

All these VB controls are placed on the form and will be used to operate the program. More importantly, these controls play a special role in the program – they are used as devices that trigger the program's action. As you know, the program's work or action is accomplished by executing a certain part of the program's code. So to initiate a program's action we need a mechanism that will tie up a certain program event, such as a key press or a mouse button click, with a certain identifiable piece of the program's code. This mechanism is provided by the VB control's ability to fire a certain event in response to a certain user action. The VB runtime system then captures this event and executes an event procedure associated with that particular control's event.

Thus, a visual image generated by a VB control class acquires a capability to function as a programmable device. Each VB control is capable of firing a set of events. A control's event will fire when the user performs a certain action using the mouse or the keyboard. Let's analyze this mechanism with the example of a click event. A click event is one of the most intensively used control events. When the user clicks on the command button internally, it produces a CommandButton's Click Event. This event is captured by the operating system and is communicated to the program to which that command button belongs. If the developer of that program has written some code in the click event procedure for that particular command button that code will be executed.

Thus, the user initiates a certain program event; a program event triggers the execution of a certain piece of program code that performs a certain program action expected by the user. As mentioned earlier, a typical windows-based program is an event-driven program. This means that a typical interactive windows program takes action only when the user causes a certain event to happen. That's why when you open a program it waits for your action. Again, the click event example is a good illustration of this concept.

3. Understanding the Program's Code

Last but not least comes writing the program's code. We coded this program using the VB development component called Code Editor. A code editor is a text editor with a few very useful additional features that make a programmer's life easier.

Figure 1.7 The Visual Basic Code Editor.

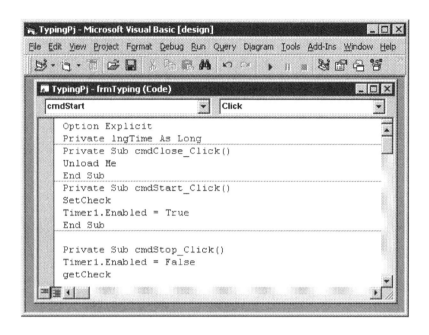

In Figure 1.7, the VB Development Program's Code Editor is shown in which you may see a few lines of code that we have written for the Check Typing Rate program. This represents what the computer gurus call the source code. It would not be an exaggeration to say that the source code is the heart of any program. In VB, all code written for the program is divided into procedures and modules. This helps to structurally organize and modularize the program's code. For example, the code written for the click event is called the Click Event Procedure and it is written in a form module.

Listing 1.1. An Excerpt of Source Code.

Private Sub cmdClose_Click()

Unload Me

End Sub

Private Sub cmdStart_Click()

Dim str as String

Call SetCheck()

Timer1.Enabled = True

End Sub

Public Sub SetCheck()

longTime = Timer

Text1.Text = " "

str = "Start typing. When finished, click"

str = str & "on Done or press Enter. Good luck!"

lblMsg.Caption = str

Text1.SetFocus

End Sub

In Listing 1.1, an excerpt of source code of the Check Typing Rate program is shown.

Here is a very brief interpretation of this code. In this piece of code, there are two CommandButton click event procedures and one independent subroutine procedure. The first click event procedure belongs to the Close command button. This procedure has only one line of code in which it calls the Unload method and passes the form object as a parameter. Note the keyword *Me* represents the active form object. The second click event procedure belongs to the Start command button. It has two lines of code. In the first line, we call the independent procedure SetCheck and in the second line, we enable the timer control. In the third procedure, we create a time stamp as a checkpoint of when the action started. We then clear the text box, change the background color of the label control, display an instructional message in the label control and move focus to the large text box. We call this procedure an independent procedure to emphasize that it is not an event procedure. Note such procedures will never be executed unless we explicitly call them from another procedure. More on this topic in Lesson 6.

The following is a selected list of programming terms used in this lesson. Please read the short definition of each term and if you have trouble understanding any then review the lesson.

A Program's Functionality   The work that a program can do

A Program's Data Input   Information fed into a program

A Program's Data Output   Information displayed or released by a program

An Interactive Program   A program that can exchange information with a user

A Program's User Interface   A program's computer generated screen

GUI   Graphical user interface

Data Processing   Information computation task performed by a program

An Application   A Program

A Visual Basic Control   A visual programmable element of a

	form
An Event-Driven Program	A program that acts when a program's event happens
A Program's Event	Any event of a form or a control used in the program
An Event Procedure	A procedure associated with a certain program event
Source Code	A program's code

Congratulations! You have successfully completed Lesson 1. If you managed to get to this point then we are sure you will make it. On completing this lesson you will have a good understanding of what VB programming is like. More importantly, you will be ready to successfully complete the whole course. Good luck!

Lesson 2

Lesson 2

How to Use the Visual Basic®

Programming Tools

In this Lesson:

You will learn how to use the Visual Basic development program to create a simple program, and how to use the Menus, Toolbars, Windows, Forms, Controls and Code Editor. Your homework assignment will be to create your fist project.

Contents of Lesson 2

Part A: Understanding the Visual Basic Development Tools

1. Using Visual Basic to Develop Programs

    a) The User Interface Design

    b) Writing Code

2. Opening the VB Development Program for the First Time

3. Practice at Using Visual Basic to Create a New Project

4. The Visual Basic Development Program Operation Tools

    a) Using the Menu Bar and the Toolbar

    b) The Menu Bar

    c) The Toolbar

    d) The Context Menu

5. The Visual Basic Development Program Components

    a) The Project Explorer

    b) The Toolbox

c) The Form Designer and the Toolbox

d) The Properties Window

e) The Code Editor

Part B: How to Create a Simple VB Program

1. Project Development Plan

2. Project Development Plan in Detail

Part C: Homework Assignment Project

1. Create and Save Project 1: *MyFirst*

2. Add Controls and Set their Properties

a) Open the Form Designer

b) Open the Toolbox

c) Set the Properties of Objects

d) The Click Event Procedure

3. Write the Application Code

a) Open the Code Editor

b) Write the Click Event Procedure

4. Run and Test the Application

Understanding the Visual Basic® Development Tools

The Visual Basic® Development Program, which is also known as the Visual Basic Integrated Development Environment (IDE), is a program that you can use to create your own programs. In this lesson, we will look at the VB IDE in general, and in the upcoming lessons, you will learn how to use each development program's component in more detail.

1. Using Visual Basic® to Develop Programs

You can use VB IDE to create a new project or work on the existing one. In most cases when you create a typical VB program you will have to accomplish at least two major types of development work: designing the user interface and writing the program's code. You need to create a user interface so that the program can generate corresponding computer screens at runtime while writing code is necessary to implement the program's functionality.

a) The User Interface Design

When you create a user interface, you will actually be doing some graphical design work. The result of this work is a visual image that will be displayed to the program's user. Most windows created by your program will be based on the VB form control. You will learn more about the VB form in Lesson 3.

Creating a proper user interface will require some graphical design work. You can accomplish this work mostly by dragging and dropping various VB controls onto the form. Once you have placed all the controls on the form you may also want to set their graphical properties such as their width, height, background color and so on.

The result of this work is a window or a computer screen that will be displayed when the program runs.

b) Writing Code

Writing code to implement the program's functionality is the most challenging part of the development work. It is also very important. You have to learn a programming language to be able to write a function or a procedure that will be executed when the program runs. Although this is the most complicated part of the work, it is also very creative and intellectually challenging work. For those of you who do not mind putting your intellects under the high pressure of creative work this kind of brainstorm may be great and highly rewarding fun. In most cases, you will write code in the event procedures, independent procedures or functions. To write code you need to learn the VB syntax and semantics and learn how to use various VB built-in functions.

Souleiman Valiev

2. Opening the VB Development Program for the First Time

When you open the VB program, it is assumed that you are opening it either to create a new project or to continue working on an existing one. Every time you open the VB development program, a certain routine is completed. You may change and customize this routine when you are more proficient in using VB. This routine has three major stages. The first stage involves the New Project dialog box. This dialog box is the first thing that you will see when you open Visual Basic. It is a very useful tool that offers you two choices: to work on an existing project or create a new one.

If you choose the New tab in the New Project dialog box, the VB will show you a set of project templates that will help you to create a new project. How does a template help you to create a new project? Most of this help is in the fact that the VB project template

40

creates a skeleton of your new project. All you have to do then is set

or change properties and names of objects used in the project. Thus,

the New Project dialog box will offer you three choices to select

from: New, Existing and Recent.

Figure 2.1 The New Project dialog box.

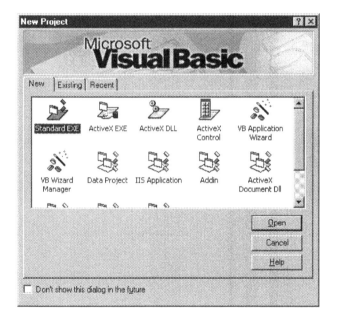

In Figure 2.1, the New Project dialog box with the NEW tab

selected is shown. Note by default the New Project dialog box will be opened with the New tab selected. The New tab displays a set of

project templates that you may use to create a new project.

Figure 2.2. The Existing Tab in the New Project Dialog Box.

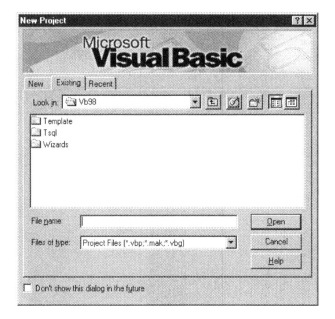

In Figure 2.2, the New Project dialog box with the EXISTING

tab selected is shown. You may use the Existing tab to open a project

that you have already created and saved in a certain directory. Thus,

to open an existing project just click on the Look In drop down box and navigate to the folder that contains the project file with the ".vbp" file name extension, and then click on the Open button. The project will be opened in the VB IDE.

Figure 2.3. The RECENT Tab in the New Project dialog box.

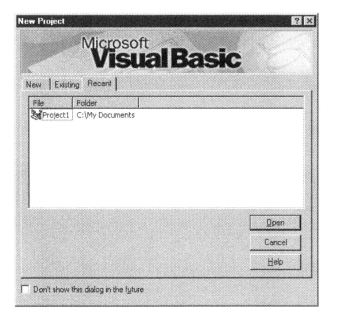

In Figure 2.3, the New Project dialog box with the RECENT tab selected is shown. It can be used to open any project that you worked on recently. You don't need to remember where the "vbp" file is saved and you don't need to navigate to the folder where that file is located. All you have to do is to select a project from the list and click on the Open button.

3. Practice at Using Visual Basic to Create a New Project

To open the VB IDE and create a new project, follow these steps:

Step 1. Open the Visual Basic Program.

On the Start menu, choose Programs, then Microsoft Visual Studio 6.0 and then Microsoft Visual Basic 6.0. The New Project dialog box should appear.

Step 2. Select the New tab from the New Project dialog box.

Normally, the New tab should be selected by default. The New tab will display a set of project templates that you can choose from.

Step 3. Select a Standard Exe project template and click on the Open button.

In the New Project dialog box select a Standard Exe project template and then click on the Open button. This action will actually open the Visual Basic development program and you should see the VB IDE window like the one shown in Figure 2.4.

Figure 2.4. The Visual Basic Development Program.

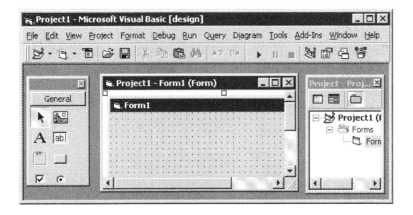

In Figure 2.4, you can see the VB IDE window with the Project1 project opened in it. Note, we have resized this window to make it compact; your VB IDE may look different. This project was created for you by VB. At this point, what VB has created is just a skeleton of a new project that includes one VB form module. Behind the scenes the VB system creates two files: the project file named Project1.vbp, and the form module file named Form1.frm. If you are going to save this project, you may want to select a directory to store these files or accept the default directory, VB98, suggested by VB. We recommend that you always save your project files in designated directories. This will save your time and will help you to organize your work properly. Now you have everything ready to start working on your new project. However, there is one problem: you need to know how to use the VB development tools and components. We will do this in the following sections.

4. The Visual Basic® Development Program Operation Tools

Learning how to use the VB IDE can be divided into two main parts. The first part consists of learning how to navigate to VB IDE components or simply how to find and open a certain development component. For example, you may need to know how to open the VB Form Designer or the Code Editor. The second part requires learning how to use the features and the functionality of each VB IDE component. For example, to design a user interface you need to know how to use the Form Designer to place controls on the form and to set their visual properties. To write code you need to learn the VB programming language and know how to use the VB Code Editor to create functions and subroutines.

To cope with the first part, you need to get familiar with the VB IDE operation tools. There are three major VB IDE operation tools: the Menu Bar, the Toolbar and the context menu. As for the VB

IDE major development components, they are: the Project Explorer, the Form Designer, the Toolbox, the Properties Window and the Code Editor. In the next section, we will explore each operation tool in more details.

a) Using the Menu Bar and the Toolbar

Using the VB development program is based on using certain development program components. To use any VB IDE component you need to open it. This task can be accomplished by using either the Menu Bar or the Toolbar. These two operation tools can perform almost exactly the same tasks. For example, you may open the Project Explorer by clicking on the corresponding button on the Toolbar or by choosing the Project Explorer submenu on the View menu. The only difference is that the Toolbar has all its tools displayed and ready to use while the Menu Bar shows one line of menus and hides all available submenus. That's why opening the Project Explorer from the Toolbar costs you one click while using the Menu Bar costs you two clicks. However, the Menu Bar contains all available functions and features while the Toolbar is restricted by its size and can display only a limited number of buttons. Note that you can customize your toolbar to include desired buttons.

Figure 2.5. The Menu Bar and the Toolbar.

b) The Menu Bar

In this lesson, we will cover only the most often used menus in the Menu Bar. In Figure 2.5, the Menu Bar and the Toolbar sections of the VB IDE are shown. The first item on the Menu Bar is the File menu.

The File menu may be used to perform the following actions: To Open, Save, Remove or Compile a project.

The View menu is used to open or hide any VB IDE component and it can be used to set certain visibility features. For example, you can use the View menu to hide or make visible the standard toolbar or any additional toolbars. Thus, from the View menu you may open or hide any VB development program component, for example the Form Designer, the Code Editor, the Properties Window and the Project Explorer.

The Project menu can be used to add or remove project files, set references, add components or set the project properties.

The Tools menu is used to add a new code procedure or function, set optional features of the VB development program and publish program files or output.

The Help menu is used to access the online help library.

c) The Toolbar

The Standard Toolbar contains a set of buttons that represent all the major project development features. For example, it may include such functional buttons as Add Project, Add Form, Open Project, Save Project, Show Toolbox and Show Properties window. There are also some additional toolbars that can be added to the VB IDE from the View menu. The following toolbars can be added if you need them in your development work: the Debug toolbar, the Edit toolbar, the Form Editor toolbar and some others.

d) The Context Menu

The Context Menu is a special menu that pops up when you right-click the form or any control on your form. The Context menu is also known as the pop-up menu. Pop-up menus are very helpful because they give you immediate access to functions and properties of the object that you have right-clicked. For example, if you right-click the CommandButton you will see the context menu shown in Figure 2.6.

Figure 2.6. A VB Control's Context Menu.

If you choose Properties from this menu, it will open the Properties window for you and will select this CommandButton from all other controls on the form. Here you can set the properties of this CommandButton. If you choose View Code, the context menu will open the Code Editor and show the click event procedure of this CommandButton.

5. The Visual Basic Development Program Components

In this lesson you will learn how to use the following VB IDE components: the Project Explorer, the Form Designer, the Toolbox, the Properties Window and the Code Editor.

a) The Project Explorer

The Project Explorer is a component that is very useful to manage all project modules and files associated with those modules. It is a window that shows a tree-like view of all modules included in this project. Not only you can view all the project modules but also you can select one and work on it. In the Project Explorer, you can navigate to the Form Designer and Code Editor windows. For example, you can select to view the form module's visual image by clicking on the View Object button, or you can view the form module's code by clicking on the View Code button. In Figure 2.7, the Project Explorer window of the Check Typing Rate project is shown.

Figure 2.7 The Project Explorer.

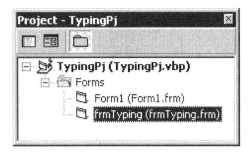

The first item listed in this window is the project name and the project file name (TypingPj.vbp) listed in parenthesis. If you expand the Forms folder you can see two form modules. Note each form module's name is followed by the form's file name in parenthesis. For example, Form1 is the form module name and Form1.frm shown in parenthesis is the form module's physical file name. If you take a closer look at the Project Explorer, you will notice two small buttons in the left corner beneath the blue title bar. The first button from the left that carries an image of a code page is the View Code button. It can be used to open the Code Editor. The button next to it is the View Object button. It can be used to bring up the Form Designer.

b) The Toolbox

The Toolbox is a window that displays a set of buttons. Each button represents a certain VB control. To place a control on the form you need to click on the control and then press the left mouse button and draw that control on the form while holding the mouse button down. The Toolbox is shown in Figure 2.8.

Figure 2.8. The Toolbox Window

c) The Form Designer and the Toolbox

The Form Designer is used to build the visual image of a program's screen. Working on the form design can be divided into two major parts: placing controls on the form and setting the visual properties of the form and the controls. To place controls on the form you need to bring up both the Form Designer and the Toolbox as shown in Figure 2.9.

Figure 2.9. The Form Designer and the Toolbox.

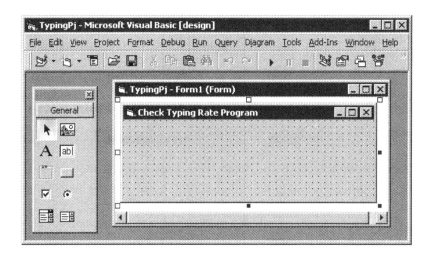

In Figure 2.9, the Toolbox is a small dialog box on the left that contains a set of controls and the Form Designer is the right window that has an empty form in it. As you can see, the Form Designer window shows two title bars. The first title bar belongs to the Form Designer and displays the project name "TypingPj" and the form name "Form1 (Form)". The second title bar belongs to the form and displays the form's caption: "Check Typing Rate Program."

Note that there are two ways to place controls on the form. You can click on the control in the Toolbox and then press the left mouse button and draw a control in a certain place on the form. The other way to do it is to double-click the control and it will be randomly drawn on the form. To move a control to a desired location you can press on the left mouse button and drag it. Once you are done with placing controls on the form, you may want to set their visual properties. To set the form and the control's properties, you need to use the Properties window.

d) The Properties Window

The Properties window has a drop down list box that lists the form module and each control that you have placed on the form. Below the drop down, there is a large pane that displays all the available properties for the selected control. To set a certain property of a control, you need to select that property and either type in the desired property value or select it from a drop down list box. The Properties window is shown in Figure 2.10.

Figure 2.10. The Properties Window.

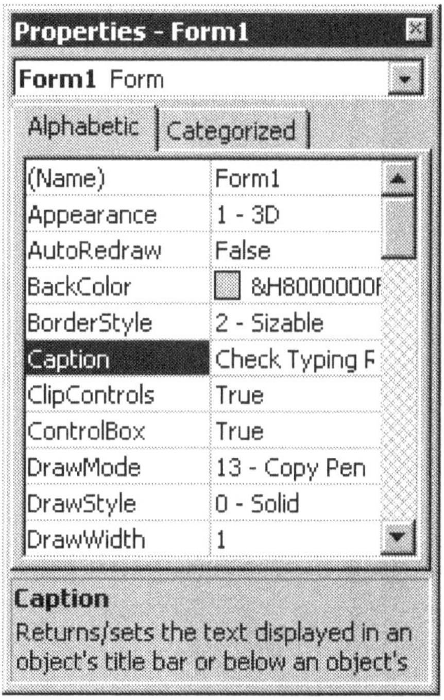

e) The Code Editor

The Code Editor is used to write code. You can write code in one project module at a time. For example, you can write code in the Form1 form module. Code that you have written in a form module will be saved in the form file. Figure 2.11 shows the Code Editor that displays a part of the frmTyping form module code. Please note that both the project and the form files are text files. This means that you can actually open and modify them with any text editor, such as Notepad or WordPad. However, using the VB Code Editor is more convenient because it has a number of built-in features, such as Auto Syntax Check, Require Variable Declaration, Auto List Members, Auto Quick Info, Auto Data Tips, Drag-and-Drop Text Editing, and Procedure Separator.

Figure 2.11 The Code Editor.

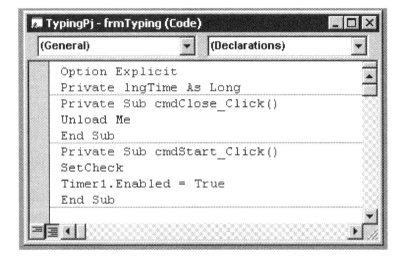

As mentioned earlier, the application code is structurally divided into modules and procedures. In each project module, you can write code in certain procedures. Each procedure has the so-called wrapper lines that signal the beginning and the end of the procedure. If you look at the code editor window in Figure 2.11, you will notice that it has two drop down boxes and a large text box. The left drop down is called Object and it displays all controls that you have placed on the form as objects. The right drop down is called Procedure. It displays a list of event procedures that are available for the object selected in the Object drop down.

Thus, when you select one of the objects from the Object drop down the Procedure drop down will be refreshed and will show only those event procedures that are available for that object. This feature helps VB programmers to write code for object event procedures. To help programmers to visually divide procedures, they are separated by solid lines.

How to Create a Simple VB Program

Now let's create a simple VB program similar to the one that you'll be assigned to create at home. We have composed a simple project design plan that has step-by-step instructions for creating a program. Please remember, it is very important to exactly follow the order of each step in the project design plan. This will save you time and eliminate undesired errors.

1. Project Development Plan

Step 1. Create and Save a New Standard EXE Project.

Step 2. Add Controls to the Form and Set their Properties.

Step 3. Write the Application Code.

Step 4. Save your Work.

Step 5. Run and Test the Application.

2. Project Development Plan in Detail

Now let's create a simple program according to our project development plan.

a) Step 1. Create and Save a New Standard EXE Project

1)   In Windows Explorer, choose the drive and create a folder named *TestProjects.*

2)   Open VB IDE and create a New Standard EXE project.

3)   Set the project name to *Test1* and the form name to *frmTest1.*

4)   On the File menu, choose Save Project As; navigate to *TestProjects* folder, and save the project and the form files in it. Remember when you save the project you will have to

save two files: the project file with file name extension ".vbp" and the form module file with the file name extension ".frm". Make sure that both files are saved in the same project directory. Congratulations! You have just created a skeleton for your future program. Now you can enhance the project by adding visual elements and writing code.

b) Step 2. Add Controls and Set their Properties

1) Add a CommandButton and a Label to the form.

i) Bring up the Project Explorer by clicking on the Project Explorer button on the toolbar. If the form is not displayed, highlight it in the Project Explorer window and click on the View Object button.

ii) If the Toolbox is not displayed, click on the Toolbox button on the toolbar. In the Toolbox select the CommandButton control by clicking on it and then move the mouse pointer to the form and draw the CommandButton on it.

.

iii) Add a Label control: on the Toolbox click on the Label control and then draw a label in the center of the form.

2) Set the CommandButton and the Label properties.

Bring up the CommandButton's context menu by right-clicking the first CommandButton and choose Properties. The properties window will appear. In the properties window select the Name property and type *cmdDispaly*. Then select the Caption property and type *&Display Message*. Note the ampersand (&) is used to make the first letter a shortcut key. Now right-click the label control and select the Properties from the pop-up menu and then select the name property and type *lblMsg*.

c) Step 3. Write Code

1) Bring up the Form Designer window.

    i)   Click on the Project Explorer button on the Toolbar. In the Project Explorer window select Form1 module and click on the View Object button. The form should be visible now.

    ii)   Double-click the Display command button on the form. The Code Editor window should appear and show the cmdDisplay CommandButton's click event procedure.

    iii)   Type this code inside the click event procedure. Your procedure should look like this:

Private Sub cmdDispaly_Click()

    lblMsg.Caption = "This is a test message."

End Sub

d) Step 4. Save your Work

To save your work click on the Save button on the Toolbar or press Ctrl+S.

e) Step 5. Run the Program

VB allows you to run the program at any time when you need to test or debug it. To run the program click on the Start button on the Toolbar or press F5. The program's form should appear. Click on the Display button. "This is a test message" text should appear in the label area. To shut down the program you can use the End button on the Toolbar or just click on the Close button in the form's controls box.

Homework Assignment Project

Create your first project. We recommend that you follow the project development plan described in this lesson. Please pay attention to how you set the name property of the project and the Form and then save them in a folder that you should create to keep the project files. This is a simple program but it is very important to divide your work into certain steps and understand the tasks performed in each step. Follow the project development plan in all your homework assignment projects.

1. Create and Save Project 1: *MyFirst*

- In the Windows Explorer, create a new folder, name it *Project1.*

- Open the VB IDE and create a New Standard EXE project.

- Set the project name to *MyFirst* and the form name to *frmMyFirst*.

- On the File menu choose Save Project As; navigate to Project1 folder and save the project and the form files in it.

Note that when you save the project, you will have to save two files: the project file with the file name extension ".vbp" and the form module file with the file name extension ".frm". Make sure that both files are saved in the Project1 directory.

2. Add Controls and Set their Properties

a) Open the Form Designer

Bring up the Project Explorer by clicking on the Project Explorer button on the toolbar. If the form is not displayed, highlight it in the Project Explorer window and click on the View Object button.

b) Open the Toolbox

If the Toolbox is not displayed, click on the Toolbox button on the toolbar. In the Toolbox select the CommandButton control by clicking on it and then move the mouse pointer to the form and draw the CommandButton on the form. Add all controls to the form according to the list below. When you finish, your form should look like the one shown in Figure 2.12.

Figure 2.12 The *frmMyFirst* form.

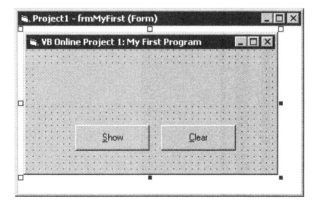

c) Set the Properties of Objects

Set the properties of the frmMyFirst form controls according to Table 2.1.

Table 2.1. The frmMyFirst Form Controls Properties.

Object	Property	Setting
Form	name	frmMyFirst
	caption	My First Program
CommandButton	name	cmdShow
	caption	&Show
CommandButton	name	cmdClear
	caption	&Clear
Label	name	lblDisplay

3. Write the Application Code

a) Open the Code Editor

Double-click any place on the form to display the Code Editor window. Note the code editor window has two drop down boxes. The left drop down displays all the objects that you have in this form and the right drop down displays the events supported by each object and helps you to write event procedures. In the Object drop down, select General. This should bring the cursor to the beginning of the code module. Type in *Option Explicit* and press Enter. The Option Explicit statement is your controller that checks if the variables used in you code are declared. Remember to include Option Explicit in all your projects; it will force you always to declare your variables.

b) Write the Click Event Procedures

Let us write the click event procedure. We will write a CommandButton click event procedure. Keep in mind that this event will fire when the user clicks on the command button. Find cmdShow CommandButton object in the left drop down list box and select it by clicking on it. When you do so, the click event procedure for this object will automatically be selected and displayed in the code editor window. You will see an empty click event procedure that looks like this:

Private Sub cmdShow_Click()

End Sub

Write code that will display a message "This is my first program!" This message will be displayed in the label control on the form when the user clicks on the Show button. Now your click event procedure should look like this:

Private Sub cmdShow_Click()

lblDisplay.Text = "This is my first program!"

End Sub

To delete the message, write code in the Private Sub cmdClear(), which should look like this:

Private Sub cmdClear()

LblDisplay.Caption = " "

End Sub

4. Save Your Work

We have included a separate Save Your Work step to remind you that you have to save your work. We recommend that you develop a habit of saving your work as often as possible. This will save you a lot time in future. It is especially important to save your work before you start testing the application because if any error occurs you may lose all unsaved code. Do not click on the Save button if you have not saved the project in a specially created folder or the VB will save it in a default directory. To save the project files in a designated directory, do the following: on the File menu choose Save As; in the Save As dialog box navigate to a designated project folder and save all project files in it. Use the Save button or the Ctrl+S shortcut only after the Save As operation.

5. Run and Test the Application

a) Run the Application

To run your program click on the Start button in the center of the toolbar or press F5. The form with two command buttons should be displayed

b) Test the Show and the Clear Buttons

Click on the Show command button. The message "This is my first program!" should be displayed in the label. Click on the Clear button. The message should be deleted. Well done! You have successfully created and tested your first program!

Congratulations! You have successfully completed Lesson 2.

Lesson 3

The Form Object's

Properties, Methods and

Events

In this Lesson:

Y ou will create Project 1, learn how to program the VB form object's properties, methods and events, write code for control event handlers, add controls to the form and set their graphical and programmatic properties, and analyze the program design time and runtime concepts.

Contents of Lesson 3

Part A: Create Your Homework Project

    1. Project Development, Debugging and Testing Practice

Part B: Visual Basic Form Object's Properties, Methods and Events

    1. The Visual Basic Form Control

    2. Setting the Form's Properties at Design and Run Time

        a) Design Time and Runtime Concepts

        b) Practice the Design Time Method

        c) Practice the Runtime Method

        d) Practice Setting the CommandButton Properties

    3. The Form Load Event

    4. The Unload Method

Part C: Homework Assignment Project

    1. Create and Save Project 2: *FormProperties.*

    2. Add Controls and Set their Properties

a) Add Controls

b) Set the Properties of Objects

3. Write the Application Code

4. Save Your Work

5. Run and Test the Application

Create Your Homework Project

1. Project Development, Debugging and Testing Practice

Create Project 1 according to the homework assignment described in Lesson 2. Please note that it is very important to practice creating a simple VB program before you continue with this lesson.

The Visual Basic®

Form Object's Properties, Methods and Events

In VB, a Form is an object that has Properties, Events and Methods. As with any object the form's properties are used to determine how the form will look like when it is displayed to the user of the program. For example, we can set the form's background color property to blue and the ForeColor property that determines the font color to red. The form's methods and events may be used to determine the form's behavior at runtime. For example, the form has the Load event and the Unload method, which can be used to show, hide or close the form at runtime.

1. The Visual Basic Form Control

The form will usually represent one of your program's windows, which in its own turn is a part of the program's user interface. The form is used as a container for all controls that you may need to use. Some controls are added to the form for you by default. If you look at the Form1 form, you will see that by default the form has a Title bar and a Controlbox. The title bar is used to display the form's caption or any desired information. To set the form's title text you need to assign the desired text to the form's caption property. If the title bar is highlighted, then the form is active or in focus. When the form loses focus, the title bar is grayed. Did you know that you could use the title bar to move the form? Move the mouse pointer to the title bar, left-click and, holding the mouse button down, drag the form. Note that the ControlBox has three tiny controls in it. They are: the MinButton, MaxButton and CloseButton. The MinButton minimizes the form; the MaxButton maximizes the form to the full screen size and the CloseButton closes the form by unloading it.

2. Setting the Form's Properties at Design and Run Time

a) Design Time and Runtime Concepts

When you design an application, there are two ways of setting the properties of objects used in the program. You may set the properties when you design the program. In this case, we may say that the properties are set at design time. For example, we can set the form's background color and the CommandButton's caption when we design the program by using the Properties window.

The second way of setting the object's properties is accomplished by executing some code when the program is running. If you want to set the object's properties at runtime, you need to write some code that will do it. In this case, the properties are set at runtime. For example, you can have the Change Color button on the form that will be used to set the form's background color. You can also write code to set the form's properties in the form_load event procedure. For example, the following line of code will set the form's background color to light blue:

Form1.BackColor = "LightBlue"

You may as well ask the user what color he or she would prefer. Get the user input, and then use it to reset the form's background color. In all these cases, we can say that the property is set at runtime or dynamically. Most objects allow their properties to be set at both design and runtime. It is important to understand the difference between these two methods of setting the object's properties. The most simplified explanation is that if a property is set before the program is compiled or by using the properties window then that property is set at design time. However, if you set the property by executing some code, then that property is set at runtime, i.e. when the program runs and your code is executed.

b) Practice the Design Time Method

Let's now practice setting some properties of the label control. Bring up the Form Designer and the Toolbox and place a label control on the form. Open the Properties window and set the label's BackColor property to green and the ForeColor property to white. Set the label's caption property to "Setting the Background color property". Run the program. The label's background color should be green and the label's font color should be white.

c) Practice the Runtime Method

Add a label and a CommandButton to the form. Set the name of the CommandButton to cmdChage. Set the label's caption property to "Setting the background color property". In the CommandButton's click event procedure, write this code:

Private Sub cmdChange_Click()

Label1.BackColor = "green"

Label1.ForeColor = "white"

End Sub

Run the program and test the Change button. When you click on the Change button, the label's background color should change to green and the font color to white. It is important to understand that the two methods of setting the object's properties apply to any object in the program. There is one important limitation. Most VB objects allow both methods of setting properties. However, there are controls that have some properties that can be set only at design time or only at runtime. The properties that can be set at design time only are marked as read-only. This means that you cannot programmatically change the value of this property when the program runs but you can read it. That's why it is called a read-only property.

One of the best examples of the read-only property is the control name. For example, we always set the name of the form when we add a form control to the project at design time. When your program runs you cannot change the form object's name. However, you can programmatically read it. For example, this line of code reads the Name property of the form and assigns it to the strFormName variable:

strFormName = frmProducts.Name

d) Practice Setting the CommandButton's Properties

Bring up the form; then shift focus to the selected CommandButton by clicking on it and then click on the Properties window button on the toolbar or right-click the CommandButton and select Properties. In the Properties window, choose the property that you want to set and click on it. Then either select a value from the drop down list box or type in the desired property value. For example, practice setting the following CommandButton properties:

Set the ForeColor – to change the caption font color.

Set the Caption property – to change the text displayed on the button.

Set the BackColor – to change the button's background color.

3. The Form Load Event

The form object has many events and methods that can be used to determine the form's behavior at runtime. Let's begin with the Form Load event. To write code in the form_load event procedure, select the Form object in the Object drop down in the Code Editor window and then select the Load event in the Procedure drop down. This is how a form_load event procedure may look in your project:

Private Sub Form_Load()

'Some code goes here

End Sub

The form load event fires when you call the Load or Show methods or when the form is automatically loaded by your program as a startup object. The form load event procedure can be used to determine what is shown on the Form and how it appears. For

94

example, if you want the form to appear right in the center of the user's screen you need to write code that does it and place it in the form load event procedure. The code that will place the form right in the center of the user's screen may look like this:

Private Sub Form_Load()

Me.Top = (Screen.Height – Me.Height) / 2

Me.Left = (Screen.Width – Me.Width) / 2

End Sub

Note that the form will not be visible until all the lines of code written in the form load event procedure are executed. So you can use the form load event procedure to do any preliminary initialization work before the form is displayed to the user.

4. The Unload Method

The Form object has the Unload method that you may use to close the form. It takes one argument – the name of the form that you want to close. Now practice using the Unload method in your program. Add one more button to your program and name it *cmdClose*. In the *cmdClose* button's click event procedure, write one line of code, which you will call the Unload method. Your code may look like this:

Private Sub cmdClose_Click()

    Unload frmMyFirst

End Sub

You can use the ME keyword to identify any currently active Form object in the program. Therefore, you can use *Me* instead of the long form name. In this case, your code will look like this:

Unload Me

Now let's test how the button works. Run the program and click on the Close button. The program should be shut down.

Homework Assignment Project

In this project, you will practice setting the properties of the form object at both design and runtime. You will learn how to use the Load event and the Unload method to open and close the form object.

1. Create and Save Project 2: *FormProperties*

- In Windows Explorer create a new folder, name it *Project2*.

- Open the VB IDE and create a New Standard EXE project.

- Set the project name to *FormProperties.* and the form name to *frmFormProperties.*

- On the File menu choose Save Project As; navigate to *Project2* folder and save the project and the form files in it.

Note that when you save the project, you will have to save at least two files: the project file with file name extension ".vbp" and the form module file with file name extension ".frm". Make sure that both files are saved in the same project directory.

2. Add Controls and Set their Properties

a) Add Controls

Bring up the Project Explorer by clicking on the appropriate button on the toolbar. If the Form is not displayed, highlight it in the Project Explorer window and click on the View Object button. Bring up the Toolbox. In the toolbox, select the CommandButton control by clicking on it and then move the mouse pointer to the form and draw the CommandButton on the form. Add all the controls listed below. When you complete the form design, your form should look like the one in Figure 3.1.

Figure 3.1. The frmFormProperties form.

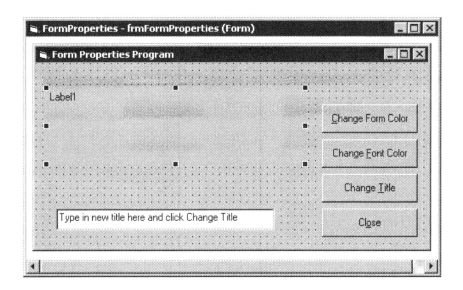

b) Set the Properties of Objects

Set the properties of the frmFormProperties form objects according to Table 3.1.

Table 3.1. The frmFormProperties form objects properties and values.

Object	Property	Setting
Form	name	frmFormProperties
	caption	Form Properties Program
	backColor	select green from the color palette
CommandButton	name	cmdChangeBackColor
	caption	&Change Form Color
CommandButton	name	cmdChangeFontColor
	caption	Change &Font Color
CommandButton	name	cmdChangeTitle
	caption	Change &Title
CommandButton	name	cmdClose
	caption	Cl&ose
Label	name	lblDisplay
TextBox	name	txtTitle

3. Write the Application Code

1.   Double-click any place on the Form to display the Code Editor window. Remember that the code editor window has two drop down list boxes: the Object and Procedure. You can use these to locate an object and select a certain event procedure.

2.   To write code for any control event procedure, find the object in the Object drop down and select it; then choose the event name in the right drop down box and select it. For example, to write a click event procedure for a CommandButton you need to select the object in the Object drop down; then select the click event in the right drop down box. When you do so, the Click Event procedure for the selected CommandButton will be displayed automatically in the Code Editor window. You will

Souleiman Valiev

see an empty click event procedure that should look like this:

Private Sub cmdObjectName_Click()

End Sub

3.   Write one line of code for the cmdChangeBackColor CommandButton click event Sub, which should look like this:

Private Sub cmdChangeBackColor_Click()
frmFormProperties.BackColor = vbBlue
End Sub

4.   Write one line of code for the cmdChangeFontColor CommandButton click event Sub, which should look like this:

102

Private Sub cmdChangeFontColor_Click()

lblDisplay.ForeColor = vbRed

End Sub

5.   Write one line of code for cmdChangeTitle CommandButton click event Sub, which should look like this:

Private Sub cmdChangeTitle_Click()

frmFormProperties.Caption = txtTitle.Text

End Sub

6.   Write one line of code in the Form Load event Sub, which should look like this:

Private Sub Form_Load()

lblDisplay.Caption = "Show the change of font color."

End Sub

Souleiman Valiev

7.   Write one line of code in the cmdClose CommandButton click event Sub, which should look like this:

Private Sub

Unload frmFormProperties

End Sub

4. Save Your Work

To save your work, click on the Save button on the toolbar or press Ctrl+S.

5. Run and Test the Application

1.   To run your program, click on the Start button in the center of the toolbar.

2. The form with three CommandButtons and a label with a message should be displayed.

3. Click on the Change Back Color command button. The form's background color should change to blue.

4. Click on the Change Font color command button. The font color should change to red.

5. Type in a new title for your form in the txtTitle TextBox and then click on the Change Title command button. The form's title bar should display a new title.

6. Click on the Close button. The form should shut down.

Congratulations! You have successfully completed Lesson 3.

Lesson 4

Lesson 4

How to Program the Visual

Basic® Controls

In this lesson:

You will create Project 2, learn how to program such VB controls as the CommandButton, the TextBox, the ComboBox and the Label and how to read and write a control's property at design time and runtime.

Contents of Lesson 4

Part A: Create Your Homework Project

    1. Project Development, Debugging and Testing Practice

Part B: How to Program the VB Controls

    1. Understanding the VB Controls

    2. How to Read or Write the Object's Property

        a) Reading the Object's Property

        b) Writing the Object's Property

        c) What is the Read-Only Property?

        d) The Object's Default Property

    3. Programming the TextBox Control

    4. Programming the CommandButton

        a) The CommandButton's Properties

        b) The CommandButton's Events

    5. How to Program the Label Control

6. Programming the ComboBox

7. Learn Programming Terms

Part C: Homework Assignment Project

1. Create and Save Project 3: *UsingControls*

2. Add Controls and Set their Properties

3. Write the Application Code

4. Save Your Work

5. Run and Test the Application

Create Your Homework Project

1. Project Development, Debugging and Testing Practice

Create Project 3 according to the homework assignment for lesson 4. It is very important to create and test the homework assignment project before you continue with this lesson. There are no additional development tasks for this project but there will be more debugging and extra credit tasks in the later lessons. Note that to successfully complete this course it is very important to create each project in each lesson. We recommend you to type all code in the project and if you get any errors, check the spelling of variables, keywords and object names. At this stage, most of your errors will be caused by typos. Read the VB error messages and follow instructions to correct them.

How to Program the VB Controls

1. Understanding the VB Controls

In this lesson, you will learn how to program some of the most frequently used VB controls. These are such controls as the TextBox, the CommandButton, the Label and the ComboBox. Before you start learning how to use these controls in a program, it is important to understand why we need them and what functionality, properties and events they have. For example, the TextBox is typically used to receive the user input.

The CommandButton is used to trigger a program's action. The Label control is used to display messages. The ComboBox is used to display a drop down list box in which the user can select an

115

item. We use the VB form control as a container to host all these and other controls. Once we have added a control to the form, it becomes an object that has a name and a set of properties, methods and events. The name that you give to a control is used to identify that object in the program's code.

When you take a closer look at these controls' properties, methods and events, you will notice that many of them have common properties, methods and events. For example, almost all controls have a background color, width and height properties. The same is true for the list of the control's events. For example, many controls have the Click and the MouseOver events. At the same time, there is always some property or event that is specific to the control. For example, the TextBox has the Maximum Length property; the Label has the WordWrap property and the CommandButton has the Default property that is specific to the corresponding control.

2. How to Read or Write the Object's Property

a) Reading the Object's Property

When we create a program we set the object's properties either when the program is designed or when it runs. We have discussed this topic in the earlier lessons. Here we would like to remind you that if you set a property when the program is designed, then you set that property at design time. However, if you set the property when the program is running, then you set it at runtime. So dealing with a control's property involves at least two major actions. Either we want to know the value of a certain object's property or we need to set that property to a certain value.

When you get the current value of a certain object's property in code, then you are programmatically reading the property. In the same way, when you set the object's property to a certain value then you are writing the property. Now let's look at two examples of reading a property. First, let's take the TextBox as an example. In most cases, the TextBox is used to get the user input. Let's say you need to get the text typed by the user in the TextBox and count how many characters that text contains. To do so, you should first read the text property of the TextBox control; then you need a variable, which will keep the property value; and then you need an assignment operator that will transfer the property value from the object to the variable. In VB, the equal sign (=) is used as an assignment operator. So to extract the text value from the TextBox control and temporally store it in a variable, you have to write a single line of code that should look like this:

strText = Text1.Text

If you need to read the background color or the font color properties used in your TextBox, then you may do it with the following lines of code:

str*Color = Text1.BackColor*

strFontColor = Text1.ForeColor

Once you have the property value stored in a variable, you can use that variable in code whenever you need it. For example, if you would like to show the text typed by the user in the label control, you can do it by applying this line of code:

Label1.Caption = strText.Text

b) Setting the Object's Property

The write property action is equal to setting the object's property to a certain value. To write the object's property you need to reference the object's property name and assign a value to it. We will discuss this question in more details in Lesson 5. Here we will briefly discuss the use of the assignment operator. The assignment operator (=) works from the right to the left. Thus, when we want to assign a value to an object's property we place the object in the left side and the value that is being assigned to the right side of the equation. Here

119

is a line of code that writes to the background color property of the TextBox:

Text1.BackColor = "Red"

When we write a property we can assign a real value or a variable that holds the necessary value. For example, in the following line of code the variable that holds the value is used to set the background color.

Text1.BackColor = strColor

c) What is the Read-Only Property?

A property that cannot be set at runtime is read-only. Most properties can be set both at runtime and at design time. However, some properties can be set only at design time. For instance, the control's name can be set only at design time and it cannot be reset at runtime. However, at runtime you can read this property. Thus, the control's name property is qualified as read-only.

d) The Object's Default Property

Any object normally has a default property. Let's say you reference an object in code but do not specify any property. In this case, the object's default property will be used. For example, the textbox's default property is Text. Note that the object's default property rule can be used in both property reading and property writing operations. Thus, to read the Text property of the Text1 TextBox we can use this code:

strText = Text1

In this line of code, we did not specify what property of the TextBox object we would like to read. In such cases, VB applies the default property.

3. Programming the TextBox Control

The textbox control can be used to receive user input or to display information. The textbox, the CommandButton and the label control have many common properties and events. We will discuss some of them.

Selected TextBox Properties:

Name – the textbox object's name.

Font – used to read or set the font type, size and style.

ForeColor – the font color

BackColor – the background color of the textbox.

MaxLength – the maximum number of letters that can be typed in the textbox.

MultiLine – If you want the textbox to show more than one line of text, you should set this property to True.

Selected TextBox Events:

Change – happens when the user types text or changes the existing text.

Click – fires when the user clicks on the textbox.

4. Programming the CommandButton

The CommandButton has a synonym push button, which actually explains its main role in an application. The user pushes the button and expects some action to be performed.

a) The CommandButton's Properties

One of the most important things about the CommandButton's properties, as well as any other control, is how these properties affect the appearance of the control. A good knowledge of properties will allow you to create rich graphical user interfaces.

Name – the CommandButton object's name.

Caption – the text displayed on the button.

Font – the size and style of the font.

BackColor – the background color of the button.

ForeColor – the font color.

b) The CommandButton's Events

The click event is one of the most often used CommandButton events. The CommandButton's click event fires when the user brings the mouse pointer to the command button and presses the left mouse button. Here's a brief description of some CommandButton's events.

The Click event – fires when the left button is clicked over the button area.

The MouseOver event – fires when the mouse pointer is over the button area.

The MouseOut event – fires when the mouse pointer is moved out.

To perform a certain action when a CommandButton's event happens, you need to write some code in the appropriate event procedure. For example, if you have the Close button on the form that is supposed to shut down the program, you have to write code that will close the form when the user clicks on that button. Write one line of code in the CommandButton's click event procedure. It may look like this:

Private Sub cmdClose_Click()

Unload Me

End Sub

5. How to Program the Label Control

A Label control may be used to display information on the form. For example, we can place a label before or over a TextBox to tell the user what information should be typed in that TextBox. We can use labels to display constant or dynamically changing messages. The label control has many properties similar to those of the TextBox, so we'll list some specific properties.

Selected Label Properties:

Caption – the text displayed in the label.

WordWrap – determines whether the label can expand to fit the caption text.

Selected Label Events:

Click – fires when the label control area is clicked.

DoubleClick – fires when the label control area is double-clicked.

MouseOver – fires when the mouse pointer is over the label control area.

If you want to display a message in the label control, you need to assign the desired text to its Caption property. Here is one line code that does it:

lblMessage.Caption = "Display this text."

6. Programming the ComboBox

The ComboBox is actually a drop down list box. It hides the actual list of items and displays one line of text. The ComboBox is used to store a list of items that may represent various objects in the real world. For example, we can store a list of product categories available at the store or the department names in a firm. When the user selects an item, a ComboBox click event happens. In the click event procedure, we may write code that will display additional information on the selected item or perform some other action.

In most cases, we program the ComboBox in the following way. We populate the ComboBox with a list of items either at design time or at runtime. When the user selects an item in the drop down list box we need to know which item was selected. We can do this by reading either the ListIndex or the Text property of the ComboBox control. The ListIndex property returns or sets the index of the currently selected item in the control while the Text property returns or sets the text contained in the control.

Selected ComboBox Properties:

Text – the text contained in the control.

ListIndex – Returns or sets the index of the currently selected item in the control.

Selected ComboBox Events:

Click – the click event fires when the user selects an item in the drop down list. Note that selecting an item in the drop down list box requires two clicks. The first click is on the downward arrow, which displays the drop down list. The second click occurs when the user selects an item from the drop down list box. This click causes the ComboBox click event to fire.

Programmatically – means by applying a program's code.

Write Property – to set an object's property.

Read Property – to obtain the current value of an object's property.

Read-Only Property – a property that cannot be set or reset at runtime.

Homework Assignment Project

1. Create and Save Project 3: *UsingControls*

- In Windows Explorer create a new folder. Name it *Project3*.

- Open the VB IDE and create a New Standard EXE project.

- Set the project name to UsingControls and the form name to *frmControls.*

- On the File menu choose Save Project As; navigate to the Project3 folder and save the project and the form files in it.

2. Add Controls and Set their Properties

Set the object properties according to Table 4.1.

Table 4.1. The frmControls form objects properties and values.

Object	Property	Setting
Form	name	frmControls
	caption	How to Use Controls in Program
CommandButton	name	cmdAddModel
	caption	&Add Model
CommandButton	name	cmdClose
	caption	&Close
TextBox	name	txtModelName
TextBox	name	txtQuantity
ComboBox	name	cboCameras

Label	name	lblQuantity
	borderStyle	Fixed
Label1	caption	Camera Models List
Label2	caption	Quantity in stock
Label3	caption	Enter Camera Name:
Label4	caption	Enter Quantity in stock:

When you complete this section, your form should look like the one shown in Figure 4.1

Figure 4.1 The frmControls form.

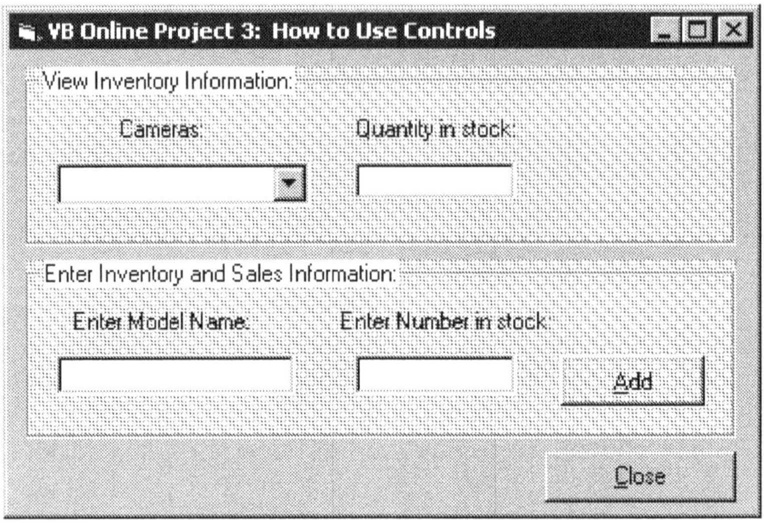

3. Write the Application Code

1. Write the AddModel subroutine procedure, which should look like this:

Public Sub AddModel()

Static iNum As Integer

cboModels.AddItem txtModelName.Text

cboModels.ItemData(iNum) = Val(txtQuantity)

iNum = iNum + 1

txtModelName = ""

txtQuantity = ""

End Sub

2. Write code in the ComboBox click event procedure. It should look like this:

Private Sub cboModels_Click()

lblQuantity.Caption = cboModels.ItemData(cboModels.ListIndex)

End Sub

3. Write this line of code in the cmdAddModel click event procedure:

lblQuantity.Caption = cboModels.ItemData(cboModels.ListIndex)

4. Write this line of code in the cmdAddModel CommandButton click event procedure:

Call AddModel

5. Write a line of code in the cmdClose CommandButton click event procedure that looks like:

Unload frmControls

4. Save Your Work

To save your work, click on the Save button on the toolbar or press Ctrl+S.

5. Run and Test the Application

1. Click on the Save button on the toolbar to save your work.

2. To run your program, click on the Start button in the toolbar.

3. Enter a camera model name and quantity in the appropriate TextBoxes and then click on the Add Model button. Check if the new model appears in the drop down list box; then select the model and check if the quantity number is displayed in the Quantity label control.

4. Repeat the operation to add more camera models.

5. Check if the text boxes are cleaned up when you click on the Add Model button.

Congratulations! You have successfully completed Lesson 4.

Lesson 5

Lesson 5

Understanding Variables and Data Types

In this lesson:

Y ou will create Project 3, learn how to declare and use variables in your application, analyze the variable scope concept, learn the Visual Basic data types, and practice creating variables and arrays.

Content of Lesson 5

Part A: Create Your Homework Project

    1. Project Development, Debugging and Testing Practice

Part B: Understanding Variables and Data Types

    1. What is a Variable?

    2. Understanding Data Types

    3. Practice Creating Variables

    4. Practice Assigning Values to Variables

    5. Understanding the Null, Empty and Zero-Length String

    6. Understanding the Variable Scope

    7. Learn Programming Terms

Part C: Homework Assignment Project

    1. Create and Save Project 4: *UsingDataTypes*

    2. Add Controls and Set their Properties

    3. Write the Application Code

4. Save Your Work

5. Run and Test the Application

Create Your Homework Project

1. Project Development, Debugging and Testing Practice

Create Project 3 according to homework assignment for Lesson 4. It is very important to create and test the homework assignment project before you continue with this lesson.

Understanding Variables and Data Types

1. What is a Variable?

A variable is a name associated with a computer memory address where you will store a value used in your program. In Figure 5.1, you can see a diagram that illustrates how the variable name is associated with the program's memory. The values held by variables can change during their lifetimes. Constants are variables that store values that cannot be changed when the program runs.

Figure 5.1. A Program Variable.

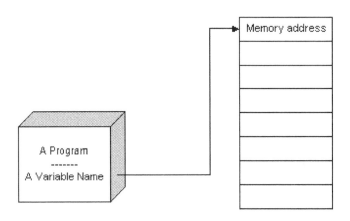

A program normally processes some data. These data can be obtained from the internal or external data sources. The program's internal data bank may be created either by hard-coding some information into variables and constants at design time or by dynamically retrieving it from various sources at runtime. For instance, a computer name, a database name, a connection string, the server name and some other information may be stored in variables and constants. If you need to use certain constant values such as coefficients or rates, you may assign them to constants at design time. The constants are special types of variables that store values that cannot be changed at runtime. As for the external data, it may be obtained from a database, a file, or another program or from a program user. All these pieces of data must be temporarily stored in the computer memory so that the program can use them when necessary. That's one of the reasons why a program needs variables. The second reason is that in a program we may need some data storage units to store dynamically changing values that are used in computation operations.

Typically, a program first retrieves data from the data source and then stores them for further use in the program's variables. All variables may be divided into three major types: simple variables, structured variables and object variables. A simple variable can store one piece of information, for example a number or a text. A structured variable can store several pieces of information or a set of values under one variable name. Such variables are called arrays. A certain single value in an array is then referenced by the subscript index. Both simple variables and arrays can store only one given type of data. An object variable can store a reference to a specific object type defined in its class. We will talk about objects in Lesson 8.

Let's summarize: in programs that you will create, you need to temporarily store some data. This is accomplished using variables. A variable is the name of a data storage unit that the program associates with a certain computer memory address. When we use variables in a program, we can either assign (write) some value to the variable or retrieve (read) the value kept by the variable. VB stores the application data in memory allocated for the program. When we create a variable we must define what data type the variable is going to keep. In the next section, we will discuss the data types.

2. Understanding Data Types

To simplify the classification of data types at this point, let's divide all data types into Numeric and Textual. For example, an Integer is a numeric data type used to store whole numbers. In VB the following data types are used to store numeric data: Integer, Long

Integer, Single, Double and Currency. The String data type is used to store the textual data.

Why do we need to differentiate data types? Let us give you at least two reasons. The first is that differentiating data types is necessary for proper memory management because each data type requires a different amount of memory to store it. The second reason is that the differentiation of data types is crucially important in data processing operations. If data are used in a mathematical operation, you have to make sure that either the variables are declared as numeric type or the values they keep are converted into a numeric type. For example, let's say you have two variables: X, declared as Integer, and Y, declared as string. If you want to sum X and Y you have to convert the value of Y to integer or any other numeric type.

The same is true of string manipulations. When you obtain a value from a TextBox control, you need to convert it into one of the numeric types if you want to use that value in a mathematical operation because values stored by a TextBox are string type by default. If your data are going to be used in text editing, they should be the string data type or you will have to convert them into the string type.

The inventory of data types in VB includes nine types. These are the following: Integer, Long Integer, Single, Double, String, Date, Currency, Object and Variant. Integer, Long Integer, Single, Double and Currency are used to store various formats of numeric data. String and Date are used to store text and dates. A few words about the Variant – Variant in VB is a very special animal. We may say that Variant in VB can potentially handle any data type. So when you declare a variable as Variant it may store any type of data. This is accomplished by a special mechanism that determines the variable's type when you assign a value to it.

3. Practice Creating Variables

To use a variable in a program you should first declare the variable and when necessary assign a value to it. Now let's practice using variables. To declare a variable use the *Dim* keyword then the variable name and then the keyword *As*. Then select the data type. For example:

Dim iNumberInStock As Integer

Dim strModelName As String

Dim curPrice as Currency

In the first example above, we declared the *iNumberInStock* variable as Integer. In the second example, we declared a variable *strModelName* as String. There is called a variable prefix and is used by programmers as an indicator of the variable data type. Thus, an abbreviation or a shortcut before the name of the variable may be used as a reminder of the variable data type. For example, the "i" before the variable name may indicate that the variable was declared as Integer. Similarly, "str" before the name of the variable indicates a string data type. A programmer may want to use prefixes to help himself to ease code interpretation.

4. Practice Assigning Values to Variables

To assign a value to a variable, you need to use the assignment operator (=). As we have mentioned earlier, the assignment operator works from right to left. For example:

iNumberInstock = 200

strModelName = "Kodak"

In the first example above, we assigned the value 200 to the *iNumberInstock* variable. In the second example, we assigned a textual value to the *strModelName* variable.

To read the variable's value, we must create a variable to which the retrieved value will be assigned. For example, let's say you want to assign the value kept by the variable to the TextBox control. Your code should look like this:

txtTextBoxName.Text = strCameraName

If you need to pass the value kept by one variable to another variable your code might look like this:

strProductName = strCameraName

5. Understanding the Null, Empty and Zero-Length String

In real world projects, you will come across many situations that puzzle or confuse you when it comes to interpreting the following three values of variables: Null, Empty and Zero-length string. In this section, we will briefly discuss this issue from a practical point of view.

When you start coding, you will soon find out that it is sometimes difficult to understand the deference between Null, Empty and Zero-length string values. I remember that I had to struggle with these notions. In fact, differentiating the notions of Null, Empty and Zero-length string is not as simple and straightforward as it may seem. We believe that the main reason for this difficulty is that technical interpretations of these notions are hard to map to common sense logic. Here's a short technical definition of each notion:

Empty – indicates that the variable has not been initialized yet.

Null – indicates that the variable contains no valid data.

Zero-length string – is a string that contains no characters.

Let's give you some descriptive definitions of these notions that may bring them closer to common sense logic. If we fail to do so, please don't give up. Continue the course.

Empty

Empty may mean that you have declared a variable but have not assigned any value to it yet. Therefore, we may say that if the variable contains no data whatsoever, it is empty.

Null

The paradox about Null is that technically Null is a value. Therefore, if a variable reports that it contains Null it means that it is not empty. It actually contains a value, which is Null. It is important to understand that Null is a value and that Null is not equal to the absence of value or to zero. The problem is that you won't easily be able to get a Null value in Visual Basic. However, you may get it from a database, for example, as a recordset field value.

Zero-Length String

A Zero-Length String means that the variable is set and can potentially contain only string data. These might consist of characters but now they contain a zero number of characters. A lot of additional confusion is added by the existence of the expression Null String or VB Null String because the Null String expression is actually used to denote a zero-length string.

Souleiman Valiev

If you want to test the water in this area of confusing terms and notions, we strongly recommend that you type the following code in a new standard exe project. When you finish typing, run this project in break mode and check the values of each variable. Before you start this practice, you need to make sure that you have turned off the Require Variable Declaration option in your Visual Basic IDE. To turn it off, on the Tools menu choose Options. Then in the Options dialog box select Editor and then uncheck the "Require Variable Declaration" check box. Now create a new Standard exe project. Double-click the form and type the following code in the from load event procedure:

Private Sub Form_Load()

'Note all variables with the "UN" suffix

' are undeclared variables.

Dim bln As Boolean

Dim intVar As Integer

Dim strVar As String

Dim objVar As Object

'Evaluates to False, contains zero.

bln = IsEmpty(intVar)

'Evaluates to False, contains zero-length string.

bln = IsEmpty(strVar)

'Evaluates to False, contains Nothing.

bln = IsEmpty(objVar)

'Evaluates to True, contains Nothing.

bln =IsObject(objVar)

'Evaluates to True, the variable is empty.

bln = IsEmpty(intVarUN)

'Evaluates to True the variable is empty.

bln = IsEmpty(strVarUN)

'Evaluates to True, the variable is empty.

bln = IsEmpty(objVarUN)

'Evaluates to False, the variable is empty.

bln =IsObject(objVarUN)

'Evaluates to False, contains no value.

bln = IsNull(intVarUN)

'Evaluates to False, contains no value.

Souleiman Valiev

bln = IsNull(strVarUN)

'Evaluates to False, contains no value.

bln = IsNull(strVarUN)

If strVar = "" And strVarUN = "" Then

'At runtime VB will translate "Empty" to zero-length string

' That's why both variables will be treated as zero-length strings.

strVar = "test"

End If

If intVar = 0 And intVarUN = 0 Then

'At runtime VB will translate "Empty" to 0

'That's why both variables will be treated as containing 0.

intVar = 777

End If

End Sub

This practice should reveal some Visual Basic secrets. First, when you declare a variable, VB will initialize it for you. You should be aware of this when you test your variable values. For example, when you declare an Integer type variable, VB initializes it to 0; a string type variable is initialized to zero-length string; and the object variable is initialized to Nothing. This can be galvanized by turning the "Require variable declaration" option off and comparing the initial values of declared and undeclared variables. The second important conclusion is that in this context using IsNull() or IsEmpty() functions to test the variable values is practically worthless because they will always return False unless you use undeclared variables.

6. Understanding the Variable Scope

The variable scope is a term used to describe two aspects of a variable: the variable visibility and the variable lifetime. The way you declare a variable when you create it will determine how long it will live in the program's memory and whether other procedures in that program can see and use that variable.

Thus, when you declare a variable you have to decide what variable scope you need. If you declare a variable inside a procedure, that variable's visibility is limited to procedure scope. Such variables are called procedure or local variables. A variable declared in a General declaration section of a form module will be visible from any procedure in that module. Variables of this type are called module level variables. When we declare a public variable in a VB standard module, that variable will be visible from anywhere in the entire program. Such variables are called global variables.

Thus, the variable's lifetime is determined by its scope. The procedure level variables are destroyed after the procedure call ends (procedure returns). The module level variables live until the module is loaded in the memory. Global or application level variables are kept alive until the application is running.

Concise Visual Basic 6.0 Course

A Variable Scope – a notion used to classify the levels of variable visibility.

A Global Variable – a variable that is visible from anywhere in the program.

A Local Variable – a variable that is visible only within a certain procedure.

A Module Level Variable – a variable that is visible from any procedure in a module.

A Public Variable – a module level variable that is visible from outside the module.

A Private Variable – a module level variable that is visible only within a module.

A Variable Lifetime – the period of time a variable is kept in memory.

163

Homework Assignment Project

1. Create and Save Project 4: *UsingDataTypes*

- In Windows Explorer create a new folder and name it *Project4.*

- Open the VB IDE and create a New Standard EXE project.

- Set the project name to UsingDataTypes.

- Set the form name to frmDataTypes.

- On the File menu, choose Save Project As; navigate to Project4 folder and save the project file and the form file in it.

2. Add Controls and Set their Properties

Set the frmDataTypes form object properties according to Table 5.1.

Table 5.1. The frmDataTypes form objects properties and values.

Object	Property	Setting
Form	name	frmDataTypes
Frame	caption	View Inventory and Sales Info:
	backColor	LightBlue
ComboBox	name	cboCameras
Label	caption	Cameras:

Label	caption	Quantity Sold
Label	caption	Total Sales:
Label	name	lblQuantity
Label	name	lblSales
Frame	caption	Enter Inventory and Sales Info:
	backColor	Light green
Label	caption	Enter Camera Name:
Label	caption	Quantity Sold
Label	caption	Camera Price
TextBox	name	txtModelName
TextBox	name	txtQuantity
TextBox	name	txtPrice
CommandButton	name	cmdAddModel
Label	name	lblSales
	borderStyle	fixed

After you have added all the controls and set their properties, your form should look like the one shown in Figure 5.2.

Figure 5.2. The frmDataTypes form.

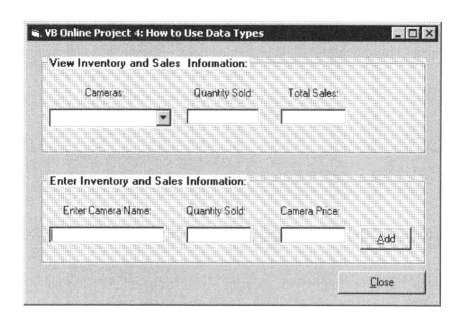

3. Write the Application Code

1. Declare two module level arrays. Your code should look like this:

Private arrPrice() As Currency

Private arrQtySold() As Integer

2. Create the AddModel() Sub that should look like this:

```
Public Sub AddModel()

Static iNum As Integer

Dim iQuantity As Integer

Dim curPrice As Currency

Dim curSales As Currency

iQuantity = Val(txtQuantity.Text)

curPrice = Val(txtPrice.Text)

ReDim Preserve arrQtySold(iNum)

ReDim Preserve arrPrice(iNum)

arrQtySold(iNum) = iQuantity

arrPrice(iNum) = curPrice

cboModels.AddItem txtModelName.Text

iNum = iNum + 1

'Now clean all TextBoxes

txtModelName = ""

txtQuantity = ""

txtPrice = ""
```

End Sub

3. Create the GetInventotyInfo() Sub. It should look like this:

Public Sub GetInventoryInfo(ByVal iNum As Integer)

lblQuantity = arrQtySold(iNum)

*lblSales = arrPrice(iNum) * arrQtySold(iNum)*

End Sub

4. Write the following code in the ComboBox click event procedure:

Private Sub cboModels_Click()

Dim iIndex As Integer

iIndex = cboModels.ListIndex

Call GetInventoryInfo (iIndex)

End Sub

4. Save Your Work

To save your work click on the Save button on the toolbar or press Ctrl+S.

5. Run and Test the Application

To run your program, click on the Start button in the center of the toolbar. The program should show the form with empty TextBoxes. Test the following functions:

1. Enter a new product. In the Enter Inventory and Sales Information section, enter the camera name, quantity, price and click on the Add button. The data should be stored in the arrays.

2.   In the View Inventory and Sales Information section, check if the item that you have just entered is listed in the drop down list box.

3.   Select an item in the Cameras drop down list box. The information about this item should appear in the Quantity Sold and the Total Sales label controls.

4.   Enter another item and repeat steps 2 and 3. If the program displays correct information for each item, you have successfully completed this project.

Congratulations! You have successfully completed Lesson

Lesson 6

Lesson 6

How to Create Functions and Subroutines

In this lesson:

Y ou will create Project 4; you will learn how to build your application logic by creating functions and subroutine procedures; you will analyze the concept of code modularization and practice using procedure parameters; you will learn the procedure scope concept and program event procedures.

Contents of Lesson 6

Part A: Create Your Homework Project

1. Project Development, Debugging and Testing Practice

Part B: How to Create Functions and Subroutines

1. Code Modularization Concept

2. Procedures are not Created Equal

3. Procedures and Variables

4. What is a Subroutine Procedure?

5. A Procedure Scope Concept

6. How to Use Functions and Subroutines

    a) Practice Creating Subs

    b) How to Use the Procedure Argument List

    c) Passing Procedure Parameters ByVal and ByRef

    d) How to Call a Procedure

    e) Practice Creating Functions

7. Procedures and Algorithms

   a) Event Procedures and Independent Procedures

8. Learn Programming Terms

Part C: Homework Assignment Project

1. Create and Save Project 5: *CreatingProcedures*

2. Add Controls and Set their Properties

3. Write the Application Code

4. Save Your Work

5. Run and Test the Application

Create Your Homework Project

1. Project Development, Debugging and Testing Practice

Create Project 4 according to homework assignment described in lesson 5. Before you continue with this lesson, it is very important to create and test the homework assignment project.

How to Create Functions and Subroutines

1. Code Modularization Concept

Let's now look at the structure of any VB application. When you examine a VB program source code you may notice that it consists of two major types of structural elements: Modules and Procedures. In fact, a program may have a number of modules and each module may contain a set of procedures. For example, an application may have three modules: one Form module, one Class module and one Standard module. By writing the application's code in separate modules, we can divide the source code into separate blocks. When you design, test or debug your application each module's code is saved in a separate physical file. This approach is called code motorization.

183

Figure 6.1 A form module code structure.

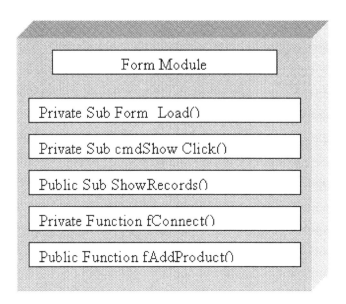

More importantly, each procedure in a module is a piece of identifiable code that can be executed by calling it from another procedure. In Figure 6.1, you can see a diagram that illustrates a module code structure.

2. Procedures are not Created Equal

Are all procedures created equal? No. Procedures are not all created equal. As you may have already noticed, all event procedures have a certain priority over independent procedures. Why? Because event procedures are automatically executed when a corresponding event happens. Figuratively speaking, event procedures are the system favorites. This is because the operating system and the VB runtime system take special care about event procedures and execute them whenever the event happens. As for independent procedures, they are left at the mercy of a programmer, who is supposed to call them whenever and wherever he or she considers it is necessary to execute them. This may give us enough reason to replace our term independent procedure with the term dependent procedure.

3. Procedures and Variables

When it comes to writing a program's code, there are two important things that you must understand and carry out correctly: managing variables and writing procedures. Function and subroutine procedures are the building blocks of any application while the data kept in variables are the application's food. To continue this analogy let's put it this way – the application procedures chop and melt the data kept in variables or obtained from the external data sources to accomplish a certain action. So most of your application coding will focus on writing procedures and managing data stored in variables.

4. What is a Subroutine Procedure?

A subroutine procedure is actually a piece of code. It won't be an exaggeration to say that whatever code you write for your program will be written it in a certain procedure. What is a procedure? A procedure is the smallest identifiable piece of code in a program. A procedure has a name and wrapper lines – the beginning and ending lines of code. A procedure has a parameter list constituted by the opening and closing parenthesis "()". How do we use a procedure? We can call a procedure from another procedure. When you do so, a piece of code written inside the called procedure will be executed.

5. A Procedure Scope Concept

A module is a home for all code procedures written in that module. So any module is a family of member procedures. Like a variable, a procedure has scope. A procedure's scope is determined by how you declare it. There are two choices: Public or Private. If you want to make your member procedure visible and accessible from other modules in the same application, you should declare it Public. However, if you want to limit access to your procedure to module members only, you should make the procedure Private. Member procedures declared as Private will not be visible from other modules in the same application.

So you can use procedure scope to determine if a particular procedure will be visible from the outside of a module. This is especially important when you have multiple modules in an application. For example, if you have two form modules in an application, Form1 and Form2, from Form1 you can call any public procedure in Form2 and vice versa. However, private procedures will not be visible from outside of those modules.

6. How to Use Functions and Subroutines

There are four types of procedures used in VB: function, subroutine, property and event procedures. We have talked about event procedures in Lessons 3 and 4. As for property procedures, we'll discuss them in Lesson 8. In this section, let's speak about functions and subs. Note that function procedures are called functions while subroutine procedures are called subs for short. Pay attention – there is one principal difference between subs and functions: functions can return a value while subs cannot.

188

a) Practice Creating Subs

Creating a sub should begin with writing the wrapper lines. You can do it either by typing the procedure wrapper lines yourself or by using the Add Procedure function in the Tools menu. The sub's starting wrapper line must include these four elements:

- The scope indicator keyword: Private or Public.
- The keyword Sub.
- The procedure name.
- The argument list.

For example:

Private Sub fSetBalance ( )

    'Some code

End Sub

b) How to Use the Procedure Argument List

As mentioned earlier, you can use the Add Procedure function to write the procedure wrapper lines for you. However, the Add Procedure utility will not create and declare your procedure arguments if you decide to use them. In this case, you will have to declare all the necessary arguments in the procedure argument list. The procedure argument list is a place where you can declare all arguments that must be passed to this procedure when it is called from another procedure.

When you declare an argument, you have to specify its orientation attribute and the data type it can handle. If you do not specify these two characteristics, default values will be used. The VB defaults are ByRef for the argument orientation, and Variant for the argument data type. To give you an example, we will add three arguments to the fSetBalance sub:

```
Private Sub fSetBalance (ByVal sAcctNo as String, _

ByVal curAmount as Currency, _

ByRef curNewBalance as Currency)

        'Some code

End Sub
```

How to Break a Code Line?

Please note that in the *fSetBalance* sub above as well as in many other places we use the underscore (_) to break the code line. This technique may prove convenient when you want to view your code without scrolling. Here's what you need to know to properly line break your code. You can break a line of code practically at any place. Just make one space, type underscore and then continue that code line on the next line. Remember, you cannot break a whole word and you cannot break a quoted expression. For example, you cannot break the following expression assigned to the *strMsg* variable:

strMsg = "Incomplete data. Please fill all text boxes and click on Continue."

However, you can use the following technique to break the above line of code:

strMsg = "Incomplete data. Please fill all"

strMsg = strMsg & "text boxes and click on Continue."

c) Passing Procedure Parameters ByVal and ByRef

A program's event procedure is automatically executed by the VB runtime system when the user causes a corresponding program event to happen. All code written in that procedure will be executed unless an error occurs or you redirect the execution process. However, in any place in a procedure you can stop code execution by using the Exit statement or by directing code execution to another procedure. In fact, from any procedure, you may call a whole chain of other independent procedures. Eventually your code execution will end up in the program's event procedure, which initially started the code execution process. In this process, one procedure calls another procedure and that procedure calls the other and so on. Thus, we will have a stack of procedure calls in which the first procedure is the calling procedure and the next procedure is the called procedure. Pay attention to the difference between the calling procedure and the called procedure – it is important to understand the following discussion of how we declare and use procedure arguments and how we pass parameters to procedures.

What does it mean to pass a parameter ByVal or ByRef? ByVal and ByRef are procedure argument orientation attributes. Here's a non-technical interpretation of these terms. A procedure argument orientation attribute is used to indicate the direction of the data flow between two procedures: the calling and the called procedures. For example, from the called procedure perspective, the data flow can be incoming or outgoing. In this context, the ByVal orientation may be associated with the incoming data flow while ByRef – with the outgoing data. Of course, this interpretation is non-technical and relative. For example, in the above fSetBalance subroutine procedure we have declared three arguments. The first two arguments are declared to have the ByVal orientation. What does this mean? Technically ByVal orientation means that a copy of the

193

parameter value will be passed to the called procedure. If the called procedure modifies it, the change will not be retained when the procedure returns because the called procedure would modify just a copy of the original data. The ByRef orientation technically means that the memory address of the variable will be passed to the called procedure. This makes a significant difference because if the parameter value is changed by the called procedure that change will be retained because the called procedure will modify the source.

How do you know whether to use ByVal or ByRef? Think about this in terms of direction. If you want an input parameter, use ByVal. But if you need an output parameter, use ByRef. However, ByRef can be used for both the input and output parameter at the same time. Note that in the *fSetBalance* procedure above we have declared two incoming and one outgoing parameter. The incoming parameters bring the account number and the amount values that are used by the procedure to calculate the account balance. The value of the new balance is returned by the output parameter *curNewBalance*.

d) How to Call a Procedure

How is a procedure executed? It depends on the procedure type. All event procedures are automatically executed when the corresponding event happens. Property procedures are executed when you reference the property in code, i.e. when you try to read or write that property. Independent procedures will be executed only if you explicitly call them from some other procedure. To call a procedure you can use the keyword Call and then the procedure name or omit the keyword Call and just use the procedure name. If your procedure expects parameters, you should create appropriate variables and pass them as parameters to your procedure. For example, in the following code we have declared three variables, assigned values to the variables and called a function.

Step 1. Declare variables:

Dim curAmount as Currency

Souleiman Valiev

Dim curNewBalance as Currency

Dim sAcctNo as String

Step 2. Assign values to variables:

curAmount = 400.00

strAcctNo = "45007234587"

Step 3. Call the fSetBalance procedure and pass three parameters:

Call fSetBalance(strAcctNo, curAmount, curNewBalance)

Remember if you use the Call keyword and pass the arguments then the parenthesis must be used. In fact, parentheses should be used in two cases: when you use the Call keyword and when you use the procedure return value. For example, without the keyword Call, the procedure call should look like this:

fSetBalance strAcctNo, curAmount, curNewBalance

When a function's return value is used, the parenthesis should be used:

IntRetValue = fSetBalance (strAcctNo, curAmount, curNewBalance)

c) Practice Creating Functions

Everything said about subroutine procedures is fully relevant for functions. However, there is one significant difference – a function can return a value while a sub cannot. That's why when you create a function you need to declare its return value data type if you plan to use it. Then in the function code you should assign a certain value to the function's return parameter. If you do not assign any value, the default value will be used. The default value is equal to the VB initialization value (for more details see Lesson 5). For example, a String variable is initialized to a zero-length string, an Integer variable to zero, and so on. Here's an example of a function that accepts one incoming parameter and returns a Boolean type.

Public Function fPutData(ByVal sData as String) as Boolean

197

Souleiman Valiev

'some code

fPutData = True

End Function

In the fEditData function, we call the fPutData function, and then we read the function's return value. Then in the If block we test the function's return value to find out if the function succeeded or failed:

Public Function fEditData(ByVal strText _

as String) as Integer

Dim ok as Boolean

Dim x as String

x = "Testing parameter"

ok = fPutData(x)

If ok = True Then

'Assign 0 to function return value

fEditData = 0

End if

198

End Function

7. Procedures and Algorithms

a) Event Procedures and Independent Procedures

Theoretically, you can use event procedures to write all your program's code. The alternative is to write independent procedures that you may then call from event procedures. Here are a few arguments in favor of the second approach. What if you need to execute the same piece of code in multiple functions or procedures in the same application module? Such code is a good candidate for an independent reusable procedure. For instance, let's say you need to calculate the sales tax in three different procedures. Then instead of repeating similar code in three places you can write one tax calculation procedure and then call it from any procedure that needs the sales tax calculation.

Another reason for writing independent procedures is that it allows a dozen procedures to be called from one central procedure, which may be called a dispatcher procedure. A third reason for writing separate procedures arises when a computation job is implemented in a complex schema. In this case dividing code into separate procedures allows for the proper organization of the sequence of procedure calls which can be combined with checking the procedure's return values and some other decision-making actions. In fact, if a computation job is a complex process, we may need to create an algorithm that will break a complex task into smaller separate pieces. In this case, an algorithm is a schema of a complex code execution process.

Figure 6.2. A Code Execution Plan.

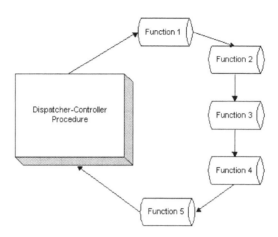

Figure 6.3. The Algorithm of a Computation Job.

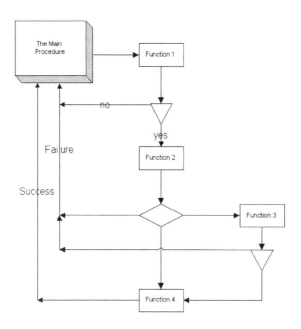

The diagram in Figure 6.2 is an illustration of how a certain program action can be implemented by a sequential execution of code in a set of interrelated functions and subroutines. Think about this as a method of breaking a job into tasks, which are accomplished by separate functions or procedures. For instance, if we have the job of displaying certain product purchase orders from a company database, we may divide it into four steps: obtain product name from the user; establish connection to the database; build a SQL statement; create a recordset object and finally display the requested data. Having this task subdivided into separate steps will, as well as having many other advantages, give us a good chance to check if each step is accomplished successfully before proceeding to the next step. If the computation job is complex, we may want to create an algorithm of the process. In Figure 6.3, you can see an algorithm that creates a more complex routine of a computation job. In both cases, if any function fails at any of these steps we can abort the whole process and report or log the error.

Can we stop or redirect code execution in a procedure? Yes, we can. How can we stop code execution in a procedure? We can use the Exit statement to stop code execution in a procedure. We can redirect code execution by using the GoTo statement or by calling another procedure. Let's say we run a decision-making test and if it evaluates to false we force the procedure to exit by using the appropriate Exit statement. There are two types of Exit statements. In functions, we use the Exit Function statement and in subroutines, we use Exit Sub. When a function or sub exits before reaching the End

Sub or End Function wrapper line, the execution will return to the calling procedure with a certain error flag or indicator if you created them. If all goes well, the execution will return to the calling procedure with a certain success indicator. Finally, the execution will stop in the calling procedure and the program will return to standby mode to wait for the next user action.

A subroutine procedure – a piece of identifiable code

A procedure scope – the level of procedure visibility

A procedure argument list – a list of arguments used by a procedure

An event procedure – a procedure that is automatically called when the event fires

A Calling procedure – a procedure from which another procedure is called

A Called procedure – a procedure that is called from another procedure

An Algorithm – In programming an algorithm is a schema of code execution process, in which a complex computation task is divided into smaller pieces and each piece is solved by one or more procedures and where propagation to the next step depends on how each procedure fulfils its part of the job.

Homework Assignment Project

1. Create and Save Project 5: *CreatingProcedures*

- In Windows Explorer create a new folder and name it *Project5*.

- In Windows Explorer copy frmDataTypes form file to Project5 folder.

- Open the VB IDE and create a New Standard EXE project.

- Set the project name to *CreatingProcedures*.

- On the Project menu, choose Add Form, select Existing and then navigate to Project5 folder. Select the frmDataTypes form and click Open.

- In Project Explorer, highlight Form1 then on the Project menu choose Remove Form1.

- On the File menu, choose Save Project As, navigate to Project5 folder and click Save.

Note that in this project you will borrow the frmDataTypes form from Project 4 and modify it. Before you start working on this project, therefore, make sure you have copied the form file into your new project directory. If you want to create this form from scratch, follow the homework assignment for Project 4.

2. Add Controls and Set their Properties

In this project, we are going to use the frmDataTypes form created in Project 4. Please do the following modifications and additions to this form and set the objects properties according to Table 6.1.

Table 6.1. The frmDataTypes form objects properties and values.

Object	Property	Setting
In the Enter Inventory frame:		
CommandButton	name	cmdEdit
CommandButton	Style	graphical
CommandButton	BackColor	light yellow
In the View Inventory frame:		
CommandButton	name	cmdDelete
CommandButton	style	graphical
CommandButton	BackColor	lightBrown

After you have finished adding controls to your form, it should look like the one shown in Figure 6.4.

Figure 6.4. The frmDataTypes form.

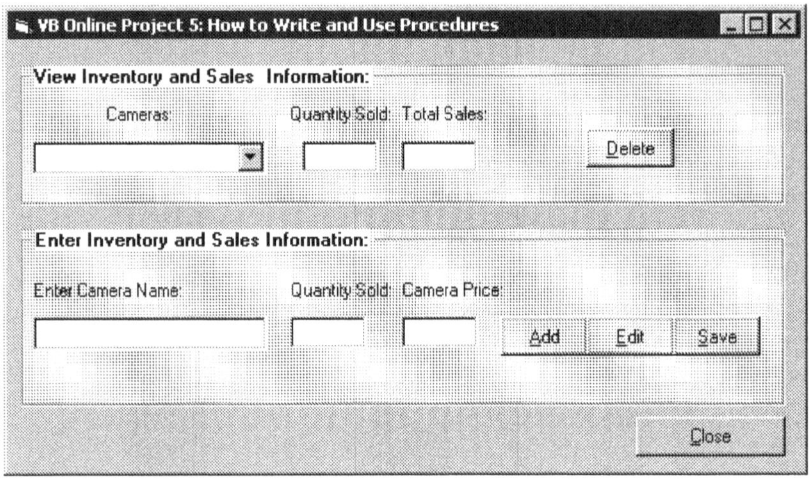

3. Write the Application Code

Note that the AddModel and the GetInventoryInfo procedures are the same as in Project 4.

1. Write the DeleteItem sub. It should look like this:

Private Sub DeleteItem(ByVal iIndex As Integer)

If iIndex = -1 Then

MsgBox "Please select an item in the drop down."

Exit Sub

Else

cboModels.List(iIndex) = ""

arrPrice(iIndex) = 0

arrQtySold(iIndex) = 0

lblQuantity.Caption = ""

lblSales.Caption = ""

End If

End Sub

2. Call the DeleteItem procedure from the cmdDelete click event procedure and pass the cboModels ListIndex value as an argument. Your code should look like this:

Private Sub cmdDelete_Click()

Call DeleteItem(cboModels.ListIndex)

End Sub

3. Write the fEdit function. You should carefully plan the order of actions for the Edit procedure. Remember the dispatcher procedure concept discussed earlier in this lesson. This is a good example of how you should control the order in which your procedures will be executed. First, the user should select an existing camera model from the drop down list box and then your procedure has to capture the selection. When the user clicks on the Edit button, you should call the fEdit function. This will show all the editable data in the three TextBoxes. Then the user is expected to make any desired modifications in the corresponding TextBoxes and finally click on the Save button to save the changes. When the user clicks on the Save button you need to call the fSave function from the Save button click event procedure. Your code should look like this:

Private Function fEdit(ByVal iIndex As Integer) As Boolean

'If the iIndex variable value is equal to –1

'Then the user did not select an item.

If iIndex = -1 Then

MsgBox "Please select an item in the drop down."

'Stop executing code in this procedure

Exit Function

Else

'This code will show Camera name, Quantity

'and Price in the text boxes.

txtModelName = cboModels.Text

txtQuantity.Text = arrQtySold(iIndex)

txtPrice.Text = arrPrice(iIndex)

End If

End Function

4. Call the fEdit function from the cmdEdit click event procedure:

Private Sub cmdEdit_Click()

Dim ok As Boolean

ok = fEdit(cboModels.ListIndex)

End Sub

5. Write the fSave function that will save changes made by the user. Your code should look like this:

Private Function fSave(ByVal iIndex As Integer) _

As Boolean

cboModels.List(iIndex) = txtModelName.Text

arrQtySold(iIndex) = txtQuantity.Text

arrPrice(iIndex) = txtPrice.Text

GetInventoryInfo iIndex

End Function

6. Write code to call the fSave function from the cmdSave click event procedure:

Private Sub cmdSave_Click()

Call fSave(cboModels.ListIndex)

End Sub

4. Save Your Work

To save your work click on the Save button on the toolbar or press Ctrl+S.

5. Run and Test the Application

1.   To run your program, click on the Start button in the toolbar.

2.   Test the Add button functionality.

3.   Check if the selected camera data is displayed in the text boxes when you click on the Edit.

4.   Check if the edited camera information is saved in the drop down when the Save button is clicked.

Congratulations! You have successfully completed Lesson 6.

Lesson 7

Lesson 7

Using the ADO to Retrieve

Data

In this Lesson:

Y ou will create Project 5, learn how to program the ADO connection and recordset objects to connect to the database and how to retrieve data requested by the user and display it on a grid control.

Contents of Lesson 7

Part A: Create Your Homework Project

1. Project Development, Debugging and Testing Practice

Part B: Using the ADO to Retrieve Data

1. Understanding the SQL Statements

2. How to Program the ADO Connection Object

a) Reference the ADO library

b) Declare a Connection Object Variable

c) Create a Connection Object

d) Set the Connection Object Properties

e) Open Connection

3. How to Create and Use the ADO Recordset Object

a) Declare a Recordset Object Variable

b) Create the Recordset Object

c) Build a SQL Query

d) Open the Recordset

4. How to Display the ADO Recordset Data in a Grid Control

a) How to Read a Single Record

b) How to Display Multiple Records

5. How to Use the *If* Statement

Part C: Homework Assignment Project

1. Create and Save Project 6: *UsingADOObjects*

2. Add Controls and Set their Properties

3. Write the Application Code

4. Save Your Work

5. Run and Test the Application

Create Your Homework Project

1. Project Development, Debugging and Testing Practice

Create Project 5 according to the homework assignment in Lesson 6. It is very important to create and test the homework assignment project before continuing with this lesson.

Using the ADO to Retrieve Data

1. Understanding the SQL Statements

In this lesson, as well as in the upcoming lessons, you will have to write various SQL statements to retrieve or modify data in the database. While far from exhaustive, the next few sections provide a working introduction to SQL. They are intended to help you understand the SQL statements. There are three basic SQL statements: Select, Delete and Update. The select statement is used to retrieve records from one or more database tables. The Delete statement is used to erase records and the Update statement is used to modify the existing records.

Souleiman Valiev

A Select statement may have three clauses: the Select, the From and the Where clauses. In the Select clause, you have to specify what columns you want to be returned. Use the asterisk (*) to return all columns. In the From clause you have to specify the table name, and in the Where clause you may specify a search condition. For example, this statement will return all columns and all rows from the Products table:

"Select * From Products"

This Select statement will return all rows with data selected only from _ProductName_ and _Price_ columns:

"Select ProductName, Price From Products"

Using the Where clause will allow you to search the table and select only those rows that satisfy a search condition. This select statement will return all table rows in which the _Price_ column value is greater than 20:

*"Select * From Products Where Price > 20"*

The Update statement may have three clauses: the Update clause, the Set clause and the Where clause. In the update clause you have to specify the table name; in the Set clause you will set the value of each column; and in the Where clause you have to specify a search condition. For example, the following statement will modify the *Discount* column in all *Products* table rows where the *Price* column value is greater than 300:

"Update Products Set Discount = 20 Where Price > 300"

The Insert statement may have the Insert clause in which you specify the table name and the columns to insert the data to, and the Values clause in which you provide values for each column specified in the insert clause. This statement will insert one record into the Products table:

"Insert Into Products (ProductName, Price, Size) Values('Bicycle', 300, 4)"

2. How to Program the ADO Connection Object

The ADO dll is a large component that may be used to establish connection and retrieve data from a data source. It has three major objects that we will use to establish a connection and get records from a database. The ADO includes the following three major objects: the Connection, the Command and the Recordset. In order to use the ADO objects in your VB project, you have to reference the corresponding ADO library in the References dialog box. Then you need to declare and create the object variable and set the object's properties. In your homework project 5, you will create a Connection object and a Recordset object, which you will use to get data from the Access database. Here is what you need to do to create the ADO connection object in your project:

a) Step 1: Reference the ADO library

On the Project menu, choose References. In the References dialog box, select the Microsoft ActiveX Data Objects Library 2.6. If you do not have version 2.6, select the most recent one. Make sure that you have checked the check box next to the library name; then click on the OK button.

b) Step 2: Declare a Connection Object Variable

In a procedure where you plan to use the connection object, declare the object variable. To declare the object variable, you have to write one line of code that may look like this:

Dim objCon as ADODB.Connection

c) Step 3: Create a Connection Object

Use the Set and New keywords to create the connection object. Your code should look like this:

Set objCon = New ADODB.Connection

d) Step 4: Set the Connection Object's Properties

Set the Provider and the ConnectionString properties of the connection object. All other connection object properties will use the defaults.

ObjCon.Provider = "Microsoft.Jet.OLEDB.1.0"

ObjCon.ConnectionString = "c:\FolderName\Filename.mdb"

e) Step 5: Open Connection

Call the connection object's Open method to connect to the database:

ObjCon.Open

When this line of code is executed, the connection to the database will be opened. If the connection is not opened and you get an error, read the error message and check if you properly spelled the file path to your Access database file. Note that if you use the SQL Server, you will have to set the Provider property to "SQLOLEDB.1" and your ConnectionString property should contain four elements: the UserID, which should be spelled as one word (you may use the abbreviation UID); the Password; the server name; and the database name. All these elements must be divided by a semi colon. Once your connection is opened, you can use it to get records from the data source.

3. How to Create and Use the ADO Recordset Object

After a connection is established, you can create the recordset object. Why do you need a recordset object? The recordset is necessary to store data obtained from the database. It allows you not only to temporarily store all the records retrieved from the data source but also to sort, search and display them when necessary.

You can create the recordset object the same way you created the connection object. Of course, you do not need to reference the ADO library because you only need to do it once. You need to declare a recordset object variable and then create it. Then you have to build a SQL query that will define what records you want to retrieve and what database tables you want to retrieve them from. Then you need to call the recordset's Open method and pass the SQL statement and the connection object as parameters.

.

a) Step 1: Declare a Recordset Object Variable

Use the Dim keyword to declare a recordset object variable and a string type variable:

Dim objRS as ADODB.Recordset

Dim strSql as String

b) Step 2: Create the Recordset Object

Use Set and New keywords to create the recordset object.

Set objRS = New ADODB.Recordset

c) Step 3: Build a SQL Query

Build a SQL query to get the necessary data and assign it to the strSql variable.

strSql = "Select * From Products"

d) Step 4: Open the Recordset

Call the recordset's Open method. The Open method takes a whole set of various parameters. To keep things simple, we can do with two parameters: the Source and the ActiveConnection. We will pass the SQL statement as the Source parameter and the connection object as the ActiveConnection parameter. Your open recordset code may look like this:

objRS.Open strSql, objCon

After this line of code is executed, you should get all the records and then use the recordset object to read any particular record or display all records in a grid control.

4. How to Display the ADO Recordset Data in a Grid Control

You can use the recordset object to perform a number of actions against a set of records stored by it. You can read the value of any single record or display all records, search for a particular record or sort the records and so on. Let's explore how to accomplish two of the above-mentioned operations: read a particular record and display all records.

a) How to Read a Single Record

You can read the value of a single record in the recordset and store it in a variable or display it in the TextBox control. When you read a single record in a recordset you will reference a recordset's field name that corresponds to a column name in the underlying database table. For each column in the database table, the recordset creates a corresponding field. So if you obtain data from three table columns, the recordset object will create three fields – one for each column. So to read a single record from the recordset, you need to specify the field name. One of the ways to do it is to specify the field name in the recordset's Fields collection. For example, the following code will store the "FirstName" field value in the *strFirstName* variable:

strFirstName = objRS.Fields("FirstName")

This is a shorter way to do it:

strFirstName = objRS!FirstName

This code will read a single record and display it in the TextBox control:

txtFirstName.Text = objRS!FirstName

b) How to Display Multiple Records

If your recordset holds multiple records, you may want to display all records. In this case, you need to use the so-called data-bound VB control that is capable of displaying a set of records. For instance, you may use the Microsoft Hierarchical Flex Grid control. This control automates the process of displaying multiple records and does a lot of hidden work for us behind the scenes. All you need to do is to write one line of code. This line of code may look like this:

Set MSHFlexGrid1.DataSource = objRS

In the above line of code, we set the DataSource property of Microsoft Hierarchical Flex Grid control to the recordset object. By doing so we delegate a large piece of work to the grid control. Behind the scenes, the grid control reads all the records stored in the recordset and displays them. You can write this code yourself if you don't mind hard work.

237

5. How to Use the *If* Statement

Here's a very brief discussion of how to use the *If* statements when you need to test a variable or expression value, check the results of code execution and direct the execution process in your procedures. If the variable or expression evaluates to true, the execution jumps into the If and End If frame. If it evaluates to false, the execution goes to the line of code immediately after the *Else* keyword, if you use it, or to the *End if* statement. For example:

If curSaleAmount > 100 Then

blnTaxableAmount = True

Else

blnTaxableAmount = False

End if

In the example above, the first line of code tests if the value of the *curSaleAmount* variable is greater than 100. If the test evaluates to true, than the next line of code that sets the *blnTaxableAmount* variable to True will be executed. If the test returns False, i.e. the sales amount is less than 100, the execution will jump to the line of code after the Else keyword and the value of the *blnTaxableAmount* variable will be set to False.

In many cases, it is important to check if the variable carries any value. If it does, check the data type and only then pass that variable as a parameter to a called procedure. This operation is called data validation. For example, you can test the variable's value by checking if it is equal to a zero-length string ("") if a variable is a String type, or to 0, if a variable is an Integer type. As an alternative, you can use a whole set of VB built-in functions to test the variable's value and the data type. For example, you can use the IsNull(), IsEmpty() and IsObject() functions to test if the variable carries some value or not. Please review lesson 5 for more details on testing the null and empty values. Here we would like to remind you that in VB all your declared variables are initialized to some value for you. For example, a string type variable is initialized to zero-length string ("")

and the integer variable is initialized to zero. This means that when you test a string variable's value you should regard a zero-length string value as the equivalent of empty.

Homework Assignment Project

1. Create and Save Project 6: *UsingADOObjects*

- In Windows Explorer create a new folder and name it *Project6.*

- Open the VB IDE and create a New Standard EXE project.

- Set the project name to *UsingADOObjects.*

- Rename Form1 to *frmADOObjects*.

- On the File menu choose Save Project As, navigate to Project6 folder, And click Save.

2. Add Controls and Set their Properties

Set the *frmADOObjects* form object properties according to Table 7.1.

Table 7.1. Objects properties and values.

Object	Property	Setting
Form	name	frmADOObjects
Label	caption	Select Product
ComboBox	name	cboProducts
Label	caption	Product Name:
TextBox	name	txtProductName
Label	caption	In Stock:
TextBox	name	txtInStock
Label	caption	Number Sold:
TextBox	name	txtQtySold

Label	caption	Price:
TextBox	name	txtPrice
Label	caption	Zoom/Resolution
TextBox	name	txtZoom
CommandButton	name	cmdDelete
	caption	&Delete
CommandButton	name	cmdEdit
	caption	&Edit
CommandButton	name	cmdSave
	caption	&Save
CommandButton	name	cmdAdd
	caption	&Add
MSFlexGrid	name	grdInfo

Note that to add the MSHFlexGrid control to your project you have to do the following: on the Project menu choose Components and then select Microsoft Hieratical FlexGrid and click OK. This action will add the control to the Toolbox. In the Toolbox click on the grid control icon and then draw it on the form. When you complete this section, your form should look like the one shown in Figure 7.1.

Figure 7.1 The frmADOObjects form.

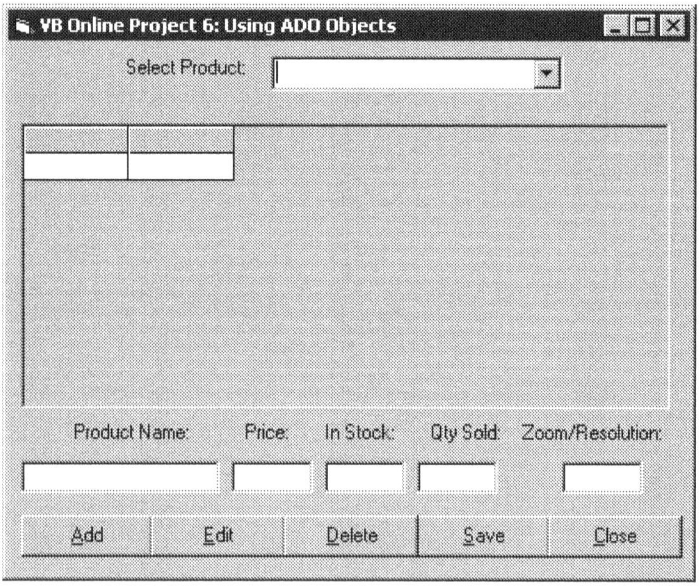

3. Write the Application Code

In this section, you will write your application code. Please note that all your work is divided into numbered steps. In each step, you will write a subroutine or a function or call a function from another function or subroutine. This coding pattern will bring you very close to real world enterprise application development practices. In most cases, your application coding will consist of writing procedures and then calling these procedures from the appropriate event procedures or other procedures. Note that every procedure that you will write for your application will constitute a piece of what the computer gurus call the application logic.

1. Write the fGetConnected function.

This function will be used to establish a connection to the database. In this module you will create two functions: fSave, fDelete and three Subs: AddProduct, EditData and ShowData. Four out of five procedures need a connection to the data source. This means that you need to create and destroy the ADO connection object in each procedure and actually repeat exactly the same block of code four times. To avoid this you may consider creating a module level connection object and writing one function that will set, configure and open a connection to the database. Since this connection object will have a module level scope, it will be visible for any procedure in your module. Name this function fGetConnected. Your code should look like this:

```
Private Function fGetConnected() As Boolean
Set con = New ADODB.Connection
sCon = App.Path & "\Inventory.mdb"
With con
.Provider = "Microsoft.Jet.OLEDB.1"
.ConnectionString = sCon
.Open
End With
End Function
```

Note that you may get this connection error: Run-time error 3706, "Provider is not found, it may not be properly installed". To fix this error check if you have Microsoft Access on your machine, check if properly spelled the provider name and the file path to the "Inventory.mdb" file that should be in your project directory.

2. Call this function from the Form Load event procedure:

```
Private Sub Form_Load()
Dim ok As Boolean
'This code will center the form
Me.Left = (Screen.Width - Me.Width) / 2
Me.Top = (Screen.Height - Me.Height) / 2
ok = fGetConnected
If Not ok Then
MsgBox "Connection to the database failed"
Exit Sub
End If
'This will add two product items to the ComboBox
cboProducts.AddItem "Cameras"
cboProducts.AddItem "Camcorders"
End Sub
```

3. Write a Sub that will be used to display data in the grid control. Name this Sub ShowData.

Your code should look like this:

```
Private Sub ShowData(ByVal TableName As String)
Dim rs As ADODB.Recordset
Dim sql As String
If Not TableName = "" Then
Set rs = New ADODB.Recordset
sql = "Select * from" & TableName
'Open the recordset
rs.Open sql, con, adOpenStatic, adLockReadOnly
'Populate the grid control
Set grdInfo.DataSource = rs
'Close the recordset object
rs.Close
'Destroy the recordset object
Set rs = Nothing
```

Else

MsgBox "Please select product first."

Exit Sub

End If

End Sub

4. Write code to call the ShowData sub from the cboProducts click event procedure. Your code should look like this:

Private Sub cboProducts_Click()

    ShowData cboProducts.Text

End Sub

Note that to refresh the data displayed in the grid, this sub is also called from the AddProduct, the fSave and the fDelete procedures.

5. Write a sub that will add new product information to the database. Name it AddProduct:

Souleiman Valiev

Private Sub AddProduct(ByVal TableName As String)

Dim sql As String

Dim sConn As String

Dim Price As Currency

Dim Product As String

Dim inStock As Integer

Dim QtySold As Integer

Dim zoom As Integer

'Read the values from the text boxes

If TableName <> "" Then

Product = txtProductName.Text

Price = txtPrice.Text

inStock = txtInstock.Text

QtySold = txtQtySold.Text

zoom = txtZoom.Text

If Product <> "" And Price <> 0 And inStock <> 0 _

And QtySold <> 0 And zoom <> 0 Then

'Build a SQL statement to insert a new record

250

If TableName = "Cameras" Then

sql = "Insert into" & TableName & "(Camera,Price, "

sql = sql &" Instock,QtySold,Resolution)"

sql = sql &" Values(" & "'" & Product & "'"

sql = sql &"," & Price & "," & inStock & ","

sql = sql &" & QtySold & "," & zoom & ")"

Else

sql = "Insert into" & TableName & "(Camcorder, "

sql = sql &"Price, Instock,QtySold,Zoom)"

sql = sql &" Values(" & "'" & Product & "'"

sql = sql &"," & Price & "," & inStock & ","

sql = sql & QtySold &"," & zoom & ")"

End If

'Run the connection object's execute method

con.Execute sql

'Refresh the data shown in the grid

Call ShowData(TableName)

'Now clean all TextBoxes

Call CleanUp

Souleiman Valiev

Else

MsgBox "Please fill all TextBoxes."

Exit Sub

End IfElse

MsgBox "Please select product first."

Exit Sub

End If

End Sub

Note that this function is written the way a novice programmer would write it, with a bunch of nested If, Else and Exit Sub statements. This is a normal logic by which your *If* tests are oriented to a positive return value but it is hard to maintain and even read such code. Think of a way of rewriting this procedure and try to avoid nested If statements and make them look for negative results. Hint, make each *If* statement check a failure condition and use the Exit command to stop execution and jump out of the procedure. You may also want to make this procedure a function and use its return value to report a success or failure. For example, the first *If* statement in this procedure may be written like this:

If TableName = "" Then

AddProduct = False

   Exit Sub

End if

6. Write the EditData sub that will populate all text boxes with data from the selected row in the grid when the Edit button is clicked. Then call this function from the Edit button click event procedure:

Private Sub EditData(ByVal selectedRow As Integer)

'This Sub is supposed to retrieve data from the selected

'grid row and show them in the corresponding text boxes

Call CleanUp()

'Find out which row is selected in the grid

'and Move to the user selected row

grdInfo.Row = selectedRow

253

'Now read the grid control column values

txtProductName.Text = grdInfo.TextMatrix(selectedRow, 2)

txtPrice.Text = grdInfo.TextMatrix(selectedRow, 3)

txtInstock.Text = grdInfo.TextMatrix(selectedRow, 4)

txtQtySold.Text = grdInfo.TextMatrix(selectedRow, 5)

txtZoom.Text = grdInfo.TextMatrix(selectedRow, 6)

End Sub

7. Write code to call the EditData sub from the cmdEdit click event procedure. Your code should look like this:

Private Sub cmdEdit_Click()

Call EditData(grdInfo.RowSel)

End Sub

8. Write the fSave function. Before you start writing code for this function, pay special attention to what is going to be done here. In the AddProduct sub, you used the insert SQL statement to add a new record to the database. However, if you need to edit an existing record

in the database table you should use the Update statement and specify the record which is supposed to be edited. That's done in this function:

Private Function fSave(ByVal TableName As String, _

ByVal RowID As Integer) As Boolean

Dim sql As String

Dim ProductName As String

Dim ZoomRes As String

If TableName <> "" Then

If TableName = "Cameras" Then

ProductName = "Camera"

ZoomRes = "Resolution"

Else

ProductName = "Camcorder"

ZoomRes = "Zoom"

End If

Else

fSave = False

Souleiman Valiev

MsgBox "Please select product first."

Exit Function

End If

If con.State = adStateOpen Then

'Check if there are values in the TextBoxes.

If txtProductName.Text <> "" And txtPrice.Text <> 0 _

And txtInstock.Text <> 0 And txtQtySold <> 0 _

And txtZoom <> 0 Then

'Build a SQL insert statement.

sql = "Update" & TableName & "Set "

sql = sql & ProductName & "="

sql = sql & """ & txtProductName.Text & """

sql = sql & ", Price=" & txtPrice.Text

sql = sql & ", Instock=" & txtInstock.Text

sql = sql & ", QtySold=" & txtQtySold.Text

sql = sql & "," & ZoomRes & "=" & txtZoom

sql = sql &" Where RowID=" & RowID

con.Execute sql

'If we got here, signal success

256

fSave = True

'Refresh data shown in the grid

ShowData (TableName)

'Clean up all text boxes

Call CleanUp

Else

MsgBox "Please fill in all TextBoxes"

Exit Function

End If

End If

End Function

9. Write code to call the fSave function from the cmdSave click event procedure:

Private Sub cmdSave_Click()

Call fSave(cboProducts.Text, grdInfo.RowSel)

End Sub

10. Write a function that will delete a selected record in the database table. Name it *fDelete:*

Private Function fDelete(ByVal RowID As Integer, _

ByVal TableName As String) As Boolean

Dim sql As String

If TableName <> "" And RowID > 0 Then

If con.State = adStateOpen Then

sql = "Delete From" & TableName

sql = sql &" Where RowID=" & RowID

con.Execute sql

Call ShowData(TableName)

fDelete = True

End If

Else

MsgBox "Please select a Product and a Row."

Exit Function

End If

End Function

11. Write code to call the fDelete function from the cmdDelete Click event procedure:

Private Sub cmdDelete_Click()

Call fDelete(grdInfo.RowSel, cboProducts.Text)

End Sub

12. Write a Sub that will clean up all text boxes. Name it CleanUp. You will call this procedure from many procedures. Review the application code and find out from which procedures it is called.

Private Sub CleanUp()

txtProductName.Text = ""

txtPrice.Text = ""

txtInstock.Text = ""

txtQtySold.Text = ""

txtZoom.Text = ""

End Sub

13. In the cmdClose click event procedure, write code to close the application:

Private Sub cmdClose_Click()

Unload frmADOObjects

End Sub

4. Save Your Work

To save your work click on the Save button on the toolbar or press Ctrl+S.

Create MS Access Database

Please use MS Access interface to build a database file. Name the database "Inventory" and create two tables: Cameras and Camcorders. In the Cameras table create these columns: RowID, Camera, Price, InStock, QtySold and Resolution. In the Camcorders table create these columns: RowID, Camcorder, Price, InStock, QtySold and Zoom. Populate both tables with a few records. You can do it either in the Microsoft Access interface or from your application user interface. Note that calling ShowData in every procedure that modifies database records is important because it refreshes the data view and immediately shows all changes to the user.

5. Run and Test the Application

The process of finding and fixing errors in code is called debugging. In most cases, you will combine testing with debugging. In this section, you will both test and debug the application.

1. Click on the Save button on the toolbar to save your work.
2. To run your program, click on the Start button on the toolbar.
3. Start debugging your application from the fGetConnected function. Place a break point on the function's starting wrapper line and then run the application. Remember that

this function is automatically called from the form load event procedure and if it fails, you will show a message box to the user that will display the connection error. When you start the application it will stop on the procedure wrapper line, press F8 to execute code one line at a time.

4. Debug the ShowData sub the same way as you did the fGetConnected function.

5. Test the application's functionality. If the above two procedures run successfully, remove all breakpoints by clicking on them and then run the application. Note that you can remove all breakpoints by using the Clear All Breakpoints on the Debug menu. On the form, select Cameras in the drop down list box. This action should show the grid control populated with records from the Cameras database table.

6. Test Add button functionality either with a breakpoint or without.

7. Test the Delete button functionality.

8. Test the Edit button functionality. It is used to place data from the selected grid row into corresponding text boxes for editing.

9. Test the Save button functionality. Its job is to update the database with the edited data.

10. Note that each procedure has some data validation code using the If statements that are supposed to protect us from various input errors. Click on each button while no data is entered to test if a message box comes up to prompt the user to enter data or select a row.

Congratulations! You have successfully completed Lesson 7.

Lesson 8

Lesson 8

Using Class Modules and

Creating Objects

In this Lesson:

Y ou will create Project 6; you will learn how to write classes and create programmable objects; you will practice creating object's methods and properties; and you will learn how to view the object's description in the Object Browser.

Contents of Lesson 8

Part A: Create Your Homework Project

1. Project Development, Debugging and Testing Practice

Part B: Using Class Modules and Creating Objects

1. Applications and Components Tandem

a) Advantages of Using Objects

2. Understanding Objects and Classes

3. The Object's Methods, Properties and Events

a) How to Create the Object's Methods

b) How to Create the Object's Properties

i) Practice Using the Procedural Method

ii) Practice Using the Declarative Method

c) How to Create the Object's Events

4. How to View the Object in the Object Browser

5. A COM DLL and Classes

6. How to Create a COM DLL

Part C: Homework Assignment Project

269

1. Create and Save Project 7: *ObjectsAndClasses.*

2. Add Controls and Set their Properties

3. Add Three Class Modules to the Project

4. Write the Application Code

    a) Write Code in the Event Procedures

    b) Write Procedures and Functions

Create Your Homework Project

1. Project Development, Debugging and Testing Practice

Create Project 6 according to the homework assignment described in Lesson 7. It is very important to complete this project before continuing with this lesson.

Using Class Modules and Creating Objects

1. Applications and Components Tandem

COM is the abbreviation for Component Object Model. A COM component is a bundle of executable code distributed as a dynamic link library (COM DLL) or as an executable (COM EXE). Before COM, an application was a monolithic block of binary code and all changes to it would be through recompilation. For example, if you wanted to add new functionality or modify the existing application features the only way to do that was through redesign and recompilation of the application. When COM came into being, things changed, opening up the great possibility of modifying applications by just replacing or modifying COM components. More importantly, it became possible to dynamically link various components while the application was running.

The term component fully describes the role of a piece of reusable code that is attached to the application to perform some additional functionality. The term component architecture is used to describe the method of building applications from components. If we take a closer look at how components look, we will see that a component is like a mini-application. It comes packaged as a binary collection of code that is compiled, linked and ready to use. The beauty of component architecture is that it offers the possibility of dynamically plugging and unplugging components to an application at runtime.

2. Understanding Objects and Classes

In Visual Basic, you can use class modules to create objects. When you use class modules to create COM applications, VB does a lot of hidden work for you. The result of this complex work is that creating objects in VB is simple. All you have to do is to add a class module to your project, give it a specific name, and write code to implement the object's methods, properties and events. That's briefly how you create objects in VB.

a) Advantages of Using Objects

Using objects in programming provides a lot of convenience and simplifies writing and reading code. Objects allow us to model real world entities, processes and relationships in a program's code by creating abstractions. For instance, we can create a *cProduct* class with such properties as Name, Type, Price and Size. Then we can add a set of methods such as *AddNewProduct*, *DeleteProduct*, *SetProductPrice* and so on. Objects hide code complexity and details behind a simple object name. If we use meaningful names for class methods, properties and events, our programming semantics will be very close to the human language semantics and will make programming great fun. All this makes writing and reading a computer program easier by actually narrowing the distance between a programming language and a natural human language. From a business perspective, computer modeling of real world processes allows the automation of slow and unproductive manual work.

Objects allow high reusability of the same piece of code written in a class, because classes are used as templates to create objects. We can use the same class to generate individual object instances, each programmed to have its own appearance and behavior. A more detailed discussion of this topic is outside the scope of this book, so let's sum up what you've learned thus far.

- Objects allow the modeling of real life entities in code by creating code abstractions.
- A class module that represents an object is a highly reusable piece of code.
- An object abstraction hides code complexity behind a short and simple name.

Objects allow us to unite the code logic and the data it uses in an abstraction.

3. The Object's Methods, Properties and Events

An object can have methods, properties and events. These three object characteristics allow us to create programmable models of real world entities and processes. Let's assume that we need to create a class that may be used to describe a dog's behavior and appearance. We create a cDog class and design it to have such methods as Bark(), Eat(), Move(), such properties as Weight, Height, Name, and such events as IamHungry() and WalkMePlease(). Thus, the object's methods are used to determine the object's behavior; the properties define the object's appearance; and the object's events are signals or messages sent by the object to the client. For example, the cDog object may send to its client application such signals as "I am hungry" or "Walk me please." The client may take appropriate action when it receives these signals or can choose to ignore them.

a) How to Create the Object's Methods

Now let's look at how methods are created in a class. Any function or subroutine defined in a class module will automatically become the object's method. The method's scope is dependent on how it is declared. As with any procedure, the choices are Public or Private. Note that a public procedure is visible from outside the object while a private procedure can only be visible to other procedures inside the class. For example:

Public Function fnBark(ByVal intNum as Integer) as Boolean

   'some code

End Function

A client program that will use the cDog object will be able to invoke the fnBark method as well as any other public methods defined and implemented in cDog class. However, a private procedure in cDog class will not be visible to the client application.

b) How to Create the Object's Properties

We can distinguish two methods of creating object properties. One of these methods may be called declarative and the other procedural. The difference between these two methods is that in the procedural method we use a property procedure that will automatically be called whenever we try to read or write the object's property. A declarative method uses a public variable to hold the property value and whenever we write or read that property we just assign a new value to it or read its status. How do you know which method to use? In a procedural method, the object's property is set or read by a property procedure. Using a procedural method requires more coding but it allows execution of any necessary code that will control the process of reading or writing a property. Why do we need to run any code when we deal with a property? In most cases, we will need to execute some code in property procedures when we want to test or validate data before the property is changed. Using a declarative method, we cannot execute any code when the property is read or modified.

i) Practice Using the Procedural Method

In a VB class module, you can create a property by using the Property Let, Property Get and Property Set procedures. The Property Get procedure is used to read the object's property and the Property Let procedure is used to write to the object's property. The Property Set is used to set a property of an object if the property data type is object. Now let's create the Weight property for our cDog class:

Step 1: Declare a module level variable to store the property value.

Private iWeight as Integer

Step 2: Create a property Let procedure in which you will take the value that arrived in the arguments list and assign it to the property variable created in step 1. You may use the Add Procedure utility that you can find on the Tools menu to help you with this task. In the Add Procedure dialog box type Weight as the property name, select Public, select Property and click on the OK button. VB will create two empty property procedures for you that should look like this:

Public Property Get Weight() As Variant

　　　'some code

End Property

Public Property Let Weight(ByVal vNewValue As Variant)

　　　'some code

End Property

Step 3: Set your property data type. Note that if you use the Add Procedure utility, it will set your property data type to Variant by default. It is your responsibility to change it to a type that suits your purposes. For our cDog class we will set the Weight property to

Integer. Remember the property Get and Let procedures should use the same data type.

Step 4: Write one line of code in Property Get procedure that will read the property's current value:

Public Property Get Weight() As Integer

Weight = iWeight

End Property

Step 5: Write one line of code that will read the value of the vNewValue property procedure parameter and assign it to the property variable. The property variable will hold that value until it is changed by another call to the property Let procedure. Note that if you need to do any data validation, you should do it before you modify the property.

Public Property Let Weight(ByVal vNewValue as Integer)

'Ddata validation code may go here

iWeight = vNewValue

End Property

Thus, to create an object property procedure you have to do the following: create a private variable that will hold the property value; write two property procedures that will read or write the property. If you want to make the property read-only, omit the property Let procedure.

ii) Practice Using the Declarative Method

Create a public variable of the required data type. Only public variables will be visible and accessible for all clients that may use the object. For example, for our cDog class we may declare a public variable Breed as follows:

Public Breed as String

Note the Weight property if created using the declarative method would also require one line of code that should look like this:

Public Weight as Integer

Any client application that will use this object will be able to both read and write to this property. Remember you have to write these declarations in the General section of your class module.

c) How to Create the Object's Events

To create the object's event you need to declare an event and then raise that event in any procedure in the class. The event can accept parameters that are actually used to pass data from the server object to the client application. Let's practice creating object events. We will now create a public event IamHungry in the cDog class. To create this event we will have to complete two steps.

Step 1: Declare a private event *IamHungry* and the str*Message* argument in the General section of the cDog class module:

Private Event IamHungry(ByVal strMessage As String)

Step 2: Raise the *IamHungry* event from any procedure in cDog class using the keyword Raise and pass a text message as a parameter:

Raise IamHungry("Please feed me!")

Please note that the object's events are something different from the object's methods and properties. The methods and properties can be invoked or set by a client application, while the object's events can be only raised by the object itself. Thus, the events are actually the only means by which the server can communicate a message to the client application. Therefore, we can distinguish two types of communication between the client application and the server object. When the client uses the object's methods or properties, the communication is directed from the client to the server. However, when the server raises an event and the client captures it, the communication flows from the server to the client.

4. How to View the Object in the Object Browser

You may use the Object Browser to view a COM library. The Object Browser allows you to look up the description of classes, methods, properties, constants and events implemented in a component. To bring up the Object Browser, click on the Object Browser button on the toolbar. In the All Libraries drop down list box, select the necessary library and then scroll down and click on the object that you are interested in; the selected object's methods, properties and events will appear in the right pane. If you select any method or property in the right pane, you will see a method or property definition in the lower pane.

Figure 8.1 The Object Browser.

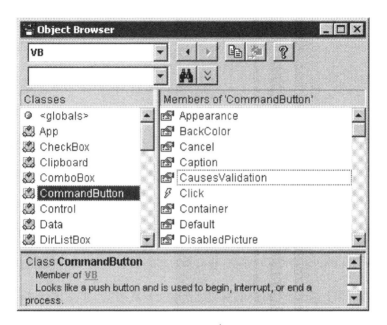

In Figure 8.1, you can see the Object Browser that shows the

VB library. In the left pane, the CommandButton class is selected and

the right pane displays all properties, methods and events of this class.

When you may need to use the Object Browser? We recommend you

to use it in all cases when you want to explore the Dll classes; the

class methods, events and properties. In your development work, you

will have to use various Dll libraries and you may need to look up the object's methods, function return value and the argument list. All this information is available in the Object Browser. In addition, you can view your own classes by selecting your project name in the All Libraries drop down.

5. A COM DLL and Classes

A COM DLL is an application that can host one or more classes. Classes that reside in a DLL may be public, semi-public or private. In Figure 8.2, you can see a diagram that shows a Mr. DLL's apartment. Classes that may live in a DLL apartment are not created equal. A DLL's apartment may include three types of residents: public classmates who can travel out of home and meet with clients; semi-public classmates who can go out but only under a supervision of some public classmates; and private classmates who are never allowed to leave the apartment, although they can play around with other classmates in the apartment.

This relationship of Dll classmates with the clients translates into the following technical consequences. Only public and semi-public classes are visible from the outside of the DLL's home. The private classes are only visible inside the DLL. Client applications can directly create objects of public classes only. However, client applications can use semi-public class objects only if the object is created by a public class. In real world, this scenario is implemented by having a method in a public class that will create a semi-public class object and then pass it to the client application.

Figure 8.2 Mr. DLL's Apartment.

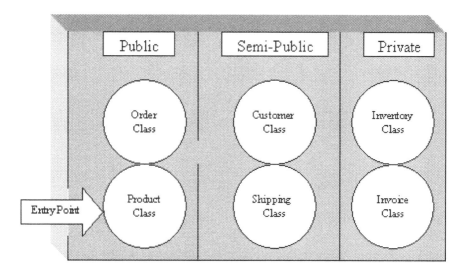

Why should there be such discrimination between classmates? Actually, it is not discrimination but rather a protection. To protect our most vulnerable and sensitive creatures, we may want to grant them a private status and lock them up in the Dll apartment. Those residents who are vulnerable but less sensitive may be allowed to travel out of the apartment under control of trusted public residents.

6. How to Create a COM DLL

In this section, we will briefly discuss how a Dll can be created in VB. To create a COM DLL application, open the VB IDE and in the New Project dialog box choose ActiveX DLL template. VB will create a skeleton of your application that will include one public class: Class1. Now your task is to design each class in your application by adding methods, properties and events. If you want to set the class status, you may do so by setting the Instancing class property. In the Project Explorer, select a class module then bring up the Properties window. In the Properties window, select Instancing and from its drop down select one of the following options: Multiuse or GlobalMultiUse are equal to our public classmate status; PublicNotCreatable is equal to semi-public; and private is private. When you finish designing and testing your classes, you will be ready to compile your Dll application. To compile on the File menu choose Make ProjectName.dll. This will compile your application and create a Dll file.

Homework Assignment Project

In this project, you will create one form module and three class modules. You will also create the MS Access database file to store the application data.

1. Create and Save Project 7: *ObjectsAndClasses*

- In Windows Explorer create a new folder and name it *Project7*.

- In Windows Explorer, copy the frmAdoObjects form from the Project6 to the Propject7 folder.

- Open the VB IDE and create a New Standard EXE project.

- Set the project name to *ObjectsAndClasses*.

293

- To add the frmAdoObjects form: On the Project menu, choose Add Form. In the Add Form dialog box, click on the Existing tab then navigate to Project7 folder, select frmADOObjects and click on Open. This will add the form to your project. Now remove the default Form1. In Project Explorer, highlight the Form1 form, and then on the Project menu choose Remove Form1.

- Modify the form name. In Project Explorer, select the frmADOObjects form and then click on the View Object button. On the Toolbar, click on the Properties button. In the Properties window, select the form object, and then select the Name property and type: frmObjectsAndClasses.

- On the File menu, choose Save frmObjectsAndClasses As; then in the Save As dialog box type frmObjectsAndClasses.frm as the new file name; navigate to Project7 and click on Save. When you finish this operation, check if the name of the form and the form file name in the Project Explorer window are the same before the parenthesis and in the parenthesis.

294

- In the frmObjectsAndClasses form, replace all references to frmADOObjects with frmObjectsAndClasses.

- On the File menu, choose Save Project As; navigate to the Project7 folder and save the project and the form files in it.

2. Add Controls and Set their Properties

Note that all form controls used in this project are the same as in Project 6. Please change the name and the caption properties of the form according to the specifications in Table 8.1.

Table 8.1. The frmObjectsAndClasses form object properties and values.

Object	Property	Value
Form	Name	frmObjectsAndClasses
	Caption	Creating and Using Objects

When you finish the form design, your form should look like the one shown in Figure 8.3

Figure 8.3. The frmObjectsAndClasses form.

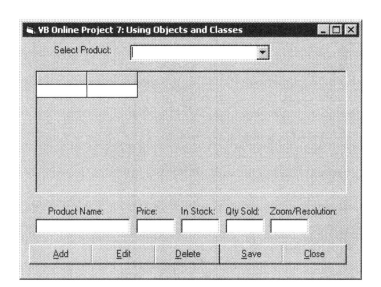

3. Add Three Class Modules to the Project

In this project, you will use class modules to create three objects that will be used in this application. All these classes will automatically acquire the Private status because classes in a Standard Exe project cannot be Public. Thus, you have to add three class modules to this project.

1. On the Project menu, select Add Class Module. In the Add Class Module dialog box's New tab, select Class Module and click on the Open button. This will add a default class module named Class1 to your project. In Project Explorer, right-click the Class1 icon and from the pop-up menu select Properties. Change the name of the class to cConnector. To save the class module, click on the Save button. Make sure that you save it in the Project7 folder – not in the default VB98 directory.

2. Repeat step 1 to add another class module, name it cCamera.

3. Repeat step 1 to add another class module, name it cCamcorder. If you have added and named your class modules correctly, your Project Explorer should list all project modules shown Figure 8.4.

Figure 8.4. Project modules in Project Explorer.

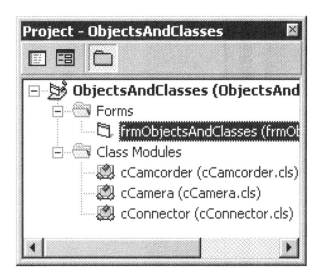

4. Write the Application Code

We will divide all application coding into three sections: writing code in the control event procedures; writing functions and subroutine procedures that will implement the application functionality; and writing code in class modules. Note that you will complete the third section – writing code in class modules – in Lesson 9.

a) Write Code in the Event Procedures

1. In the General section, write Option Explicit. Then declare two module level object variables that will represent two objects implemented in cCamera and cCamcorder class modules. Your code should look like this:

Option Explicit

Private objCameras As New cCamera

Private objCamcorders As New cCamcorder

2. Write code in the cboProducts ComboBox click event procedure.

Private Sub cboProducts_Click()

    Call

End Sub

3. Write code in the Add button click event procedure:

Private Sub cmdAdd_Click()

    Call AddProduct

End Sub

4. Write code in the Close button click event procedure:

Private Sub cmdClose_Click()

    Unload frmObjectsAndClasses

End Sub

5. Write code in the Delete button click event procedure:

Private Sub cmdDelete_Click()

Dim DBRowID As Integer

'Check if a row was selected in the grid

If CheckProductAndRowID <> 0 Then

    Exit Sub

End If

'Determine which row to delete

DBRowID = grdInfo.TextMatrix(grdInfo.RowSel, 0)

Select Case cboProducts.Text

Case "Cameras"

objCameras.fDelete DBRowID

Case "Camcorders"

objCamcorders.fDelete DBRowID

End Select

Call ShowRecords

End Sub

6. Write code in the Edit button click event procedure:

Private Sub cmdEdit_Click()

 Call EditData

End Sub

7. Write code in the Save button click event procedure:

Private Sub cmdSave_Click()

Dim RowID As Integer

If CheckProductAndRowID <> 0 Then

Exit Sub

End If

RowID = grdInfo.TextMatrix(grdInfo.RowSel, 0)

Select Case cboProducts.Text

Case "Cameras"

Call objCameras.fSave (RowID, txtProductName, _

txtPrice, txtInstock, txtQtySold, txtZoom)

Case "Camcorders"

Call objCamcorders.fSave(RowID, txtProductName, _

txtPrice, txtInstock, txtQtySold, txtZoom)

End Select

Call ShowRecords

End Sub

8. Write code in the Form load event procedure:

Private Sub Form_Load()

Dim ok As Boolean

'This code will center the form.

Me.Left = (Screen.Width - Me.Width) / 2

Me.Top = (Screen.Height - Me.Height) / 2

'Add two product items to the ComboBox

cboProducts.AddItem "Cameras"

cboProducts.AddItem "Camcorders"

End Sub

b) Write Procedures and Functions

1. Write the AddProduct and the ShowRecords procedures.

Please note that we will use the term procedure to refer to both functions and subroutines. If we classify our functions and subroutines into service and work procedures, in this module we will have two service procedures. The rest will be work procedures. Let's agree that what we call a service procedure will be a procedure that does some general tasks, such as clean up, check some property and so on. A work procedure will perform a more specific task. For example, it may add a new product record or edit an existing product record. Thus the CleanUp() and CheckProductAndRowID should be considered service procedures while the AddProduct procedure is a work procedure.

Private Sub AddProduct()

Dim ok As Boolean

If cboProducts.Text = "" Then

MsgBox "Please select product first."

Exit Sub

End If

If txtProductName <> "" And txtPrice <> "" _

And txtInstock <> "" And txtQtySold <> "" _

And txtZoom <> "" Then

'Check if there are values in text boxes

Select Case cboProducts.Text

Souleiman Valiev

Case "Cameras"

ok = objCameras.AddCamera(txtProductName, txtPrice,_

txtInstock, txtQtySold, txtZoom)

Case "Camcorders"

ok = objCamcorders.AddCamcorder(txtProductName, _

txtPrice, txtInstock, txtQtySold, txtZoom)

End Select

Call CleanUp

Call ShowRecords

Else

MsgBox "Incomplete data. Please fill all TextBoxes."

Exit Sub

End If

End Sub

Private Sub ShowRecords()

Dim rs As ADODB.Recordset

Select Case cboProducts.Text

Case "Cameras"

Call objCameras.ShowData(rs)

Case "Camcorders"

Call objCamcorders.ShowData(rs)

End Select

Set grdInfo.DataSource = rs

End Sub

2. Write code in the EditData procedure:

Private Sub EditData()

'Copy data from the selected

'grid row to the text boxes

Dim selectedRow As Integer

'Check if product was selected

If CheckProductAndRowID <> 0 Then

Exit Sub

End If

Call CleanUp

'Find out which grid row is selected

selectedRow = grdInfo.RowSel

'Move to the selected row

grdInfo.Row = selectedRow

'Read the grid row columns values

txtProductName.Text = grdInfo.TextMatrix(selectedRow, 1)

txtPrice.Text = grdInfo.TextMatrix(selectedRow, 2)

txtInstock.Text = grdInfo.TextMatrix(selectedRow, 3)

txtQtySold.Text = grdInfo.TextMatrix(selectedRow, 4)

txtZoom.Text = grdInfo.TextMatrix(selectedRow, 5)

End Sub

3. Write the CleanUp procedure.

Why do we need to write a separate procedure to clean up all text boxes? Please review the code and find out how many times and from how many procedures we call the CleanUp procedure. If we did not write a separate procedure, we would have to write exactly the same code in all procedures that need to cleanup after themselves. Instead, we will write code for this procedure only once and reuse it.

Private Sub CleanUp()

   txtProductName.Text = ""

   txtPrice.Text = ""

   txtInstock.Text = ""

   txtQtySold.Text = ""

   txtZoom.Text = ""

End Sub

4. Write the CheckProductandRowID procedure.

Note that when we started using the CheckProductandRowID function we removed some of the logic from several work procedures to it. Now the CheckProductandRowID procedure checks if both a product and a row are selected. If they are not, it shows a message box with a corresponding error message and exits. In a work procedure, we just call the CheckProductandRowID and check if the function succeeds (returns a success code = 0) or fails (returns a value greater than zero). If the function fails, we exit the procedure which called the function.

Private Function CheckProductAndRowID() As Integer

If cboProducts.Text = "" Then

'Reports error: product not selected

CheckProductAndRowID = 1

MsgBox "Please select product first."

Exit Function

If grdInfo.RowSel = 0 Then

'Error: product and row not selected

CheckProductAndRowID = 2

MsgBox "Please select product and row first."

Exit Function

End If

Else

If grdInfo.RowSel = 0 Then

'Reports error: row not selected

CheckProductAndRowID = 3

MsgBox "Please select Row first."

Exit Function

Else

'Reports success

CheckProductAndRowID = 0

End If

End If

End Function

After you finish coding, spend some time to compare code in the frmADOObjects and in the frmObjectsAndClasses form modules. You will notice that a lot of inventory items related logic is gone and managing objects from the frmObjectsAndClasses form module is simplified. Especially compare the code in the AddProduct and fSave functions in both forms. Note that there is no testing task in this project because we did not complete the project design. You will test the application in the next lesson when you complete the project.

Congratulations! You have successfully completed Lesson 8.

Lesson 9

Lesson 9

Binding COM Servers to

Client Applications

In this Lesson:

You will create the first part of Project 7; you will learn how to link COM servers to client applications; and you will learn and practice two methods of object binding.

Contents of Lesson 9

Part A: Create Your Homework Project

1. Project Development, Debugging and Testing Practice

Part B: Binding COM Servers to Client Applications

1. Understanding Object Binding

2. Two Methods of Object Binding

i) Early Binding

ii) Late Binding

3. Practice Object Binding Techniques

4. Learn Programming Terms

Part C: Homework Assignment Project

1. Complete Project 7: *ObjectsAndClasses*

2. Write Code in Each Class Module

a) Write code in the cCamera class module

b) Write code in the cCamcorder class module

c) Write code in the cConnector class module

3. Run and Test the Application

a) Foolproof Testing

b) Application Functionality Testing

c) Bugs Known to Dwell in this Application

d) The Delete Button Bug

e) The Edit Button Bug

f) How to Catch the Bugs

Create Your Homework Project

1. Project Development, Debugging and Testing Practice

Create Project 7 according to the homework assignment described in Lesson 8. It is very important to complete this project before continuing with this lesson.

Binding COM Servers to Client Applications

1. Understanding Object Binding

An object is actually a part of something called ActiveX or COM, which we discussed in Lesson 8. There are three types of ActiveX: ActiveX dll, ActiveX exe and ActiveX control (ocx). In this lesson, we will consider an ActiveX dll or COM dll from the point of view of how it can be linked to a client application.

A COM object is not just a piece of code; it is a well-organized and highly reusable piece of code, which makes it a component. As a component, a COM object is designed so that it can be linked and used by applications that support COM standard. This makes a component something that can be compared to a plug-in.

Thus, an object can be used by linking it to an executable program. The term plug-in is widely used and it is actually a good definition of what we do when we link an object to a client application.

Figure 9.1. Loading a Component into Application Memory.

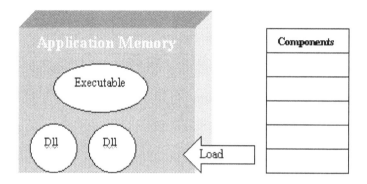

Technically, an application can successfully link a COM component only if it properly loads an appropriate Dll file into its memory space. Figure 9.1 is an illustration of this process. To better understand how a client application uses a linked COM object, we need to define the roles played by each party in this scenario. The application that uses an object plays the role of a client and henceforth is called a Client Application. The object used by the client application is a server, and thus acquires the title COM Server.

Finally, the process of linking a COM object to a client application is called Object Binding.

To summarize, let's point out that to be able to use a COM object you have to bind it to the client application. There are two types of binding: early binding and late binding. In the following section, you'll find a brief description of each type.

2. Two Methods of Object Binding

a) Early Binding

In early binding, we declare an object variable as a specific class by using COM dll program name (ProgID) and a specific class name. For example:

Dim myFavariteCamera as Cameras.cCamera

In the above example the *Cameras* is the program ID of the Dll and the *cCamera* is the class name. This method of object variable declaration allows the VB compiler to obtain the object's class ID at design time. Then at runtime the program creates the object right away and is ready to invoke its methods. So we may as well define this method as partially completed at design time.

b) Late Binding

In late binding, we declare an object variable as a generic class. It means we declare an object variable literally as an object, meaning that practically any object can be created. Thus, your object variable declaration for late binding should look like this:

Dim myFavariteCamera as Object

It is obvious that at the point of variable declaration, we do not tell the application what object it must create. Thus, we make the program blind as to what object to create until it reaches the line of code that actually creates the object using the "SET" statement:

Set myFavariteCamera = New Cameras.cCamera

Therefore, the application delays the object creation task to the time when it executes the "Set" statement, which obviously happens when the program is running. It is only then that the program first obtains the object's class ID and then creates the object. That's why late binding is significantly slower than early binding.

3. Practice Object Binding Techniques

Step 1: Reference the COM dll library. On the Project menu choose References and select and check the necessary library.

Step 2: Declare an object variable.

For Early Binding:

a) If you create an object from a private class in a standard exe project, use only the class name:

Dim myFavariteCamera as cCamera

b) If you need to create an object of a public class, which is compiled into a Dll, your declaration should include the Dll name and the class name:

Dim myFavariteCamera as Cameras.cCamera

c) You can combine the declaration of the object variable and the Set statement in one statement. If you use this method, you don't need to use step 3. In this case, the object will be created when the object variable is first referenced in code. Note that you will use this method in Project 7. This type of object declaration should look like this:

Dim myFavariteCamera as New cCamera

Or

Dim myFavariteCamera as New Cameras.cCamera

For Late Binding:

Declare an object variable as a generic class. This means that we must declare the object as an *Object* type:

Dim myPCCamera as Object

Step 3: Create the object by using the Set statement:

Set myPCCamera = New Cameras.cCamera

Step 4: Use the object in your code.

Using the object in code means that now you have a privilege to invoke its public methods or set its public properties.

Step 5: Destroy the object.

It is very important to properly manage the object's lifetime. By lifetime, we mean the period between the object creation and destruction. In most cases, the object is created when you execute the Set statement. The object will be destroyed when you execute the "Set" equal to "Nothing" statement. Your object destruction code may look like this:

Set myPCCamera = Nothing

A programmer has to take special care to destroy the object as soon as he or she does need it. This topic is huge and is outside the scope of this course. So, let us give you at least one hint. If you run your COM object under MTS or COM+, it is good practice to create the object as early as possible and destroy it as soon as possible.

A Plug-in - a COM dll that can be used in an application

Early binding - object linking that is partially completed at design time.

Late binding - object linking that occurs at runtime.

A COM - Component object model (ActiveX, OLE)

A COM server - an object linked to a client application.

A Client application - an application that uses an object.

Homework Assignment Project

In this homework assignment project, you will complete Project 7, which you began in Lesson 8. In this lesson, you will write code to create procedures in three class modules that were created in the previous lesson.

1. Complete Project 7: *ObjectsAndClasses*

- In the VB IDE, open the *ObjectsAndClasses* project in located Project 7 folder.

2. Write Code in Each Class Module

a) Write the following code in the cCamera class module.

1. Write this code in the General section of the class module:

Option Explicit

Private objCon As New cConnector

Private Resol As Single

2. Write the ShowData function:

Public Function ShowData(ByRef rs As _

ADODB.Recordset) As Boolean

Dim pRs As ADODB.Recordset

Dim sql As String

Dim ok As Boolean

*sql = "Select * from Cameras"*

ok = objCon.GetData(sql, pRs)

If ok = True Then

    Set rs = pRs

    ShowData = True

Else

    ShowData = False

End If

End Function

3. Write the AddCamera function:

Public Function AddCamera(ByVal Product As String, _

ByVal Price As Currency, ByVal inStock As Integer, _

ByVal QtySold As Integer, _

ByVal Resolution As Single) As Boolean

Dim ok As Boolean

333

Souleiman Valiev

Dim sql As String

AddCamera = False

'Build a SQL statement to insert a

'new record to the database

sql = "Insert into Cameras"

sql = sql &" (Camera, Price, Instock, QtySold, Resolution)"

sql = sql &" Values(" & "''" & Product & "''"

sql = sql &"," & Price & "," & inStock & ","

sql = sql & QtySold &"," & Resolution & ")"

'Run the ExecuteQuery method

ok = objCon.ExecuteQuery(sql)

If ok = True Then

    AddCamera = True

End If

End Function

    4. Write the fDelete function:

Public Function fDelete(ByVal RowID As Integer) As Boolean

Dim sql As String

Dim ok As Boolean

sql = "Delete From Cameras Where RowID=" & RowID

ok = objCon.ExecuteQuery(sql)

If ok Then

　　　fDelete = True

Else

　　　fDelete = False

End If

End Function

5. Write the fSave function:

Public Function fSave(ByVal RowID As Integer, _

ByVal Product As String, ByVal Price As Currency, _

ByVal inStock As Integer, ByVal QtySold As Integer, _

ByVal Resolution As Single) As Boolean

Souleiman Valiev

Dim sql As String

Dim ok As Boolean

'build a query string

sql = "Update Cameras Set"

sql = sql &" Camera=" & """ & Product & """

sql = sql &", Price=" & Price

sql = sql &", Instock=" & inStock

sql = sql &", QtySold=" & QtySold

sql = sql &", Resolution=" & Resolution

sql = sql &" Where RowID=" & RowID

ok = objCon.ExecuteQuery(sql)

If ok Then

'Signal success

fSave = True

Else

fSave = False

End If

End Function

6. Write the Resolution property procedures:

Public Property Get Resolution() As Single

   Resolution = Resol

End Property

Public Property Let Resolution(ByVal vNewValue As Single)

Resol = vNewValue

End Property

b) Write the following code in the cCamcorder class module.

   1. Write this code in the General section of the class module:

Option Explicit

Private objCon As New cConnector

   2. Write the ShowData function:

Souleiman Valiev

Public Function ShowData(ByRef rs As _

ADODB.Recordset) As Boolean

Dim pRs As ADODB.Recordset

Dim sql As String

Dim ok As Boolean

*sql = "Select * from Camcorders"*

ok = objCon.GetData(sql, pRs)

If ok = True Then

Set rs = pRs

ShowData = True

Else

ShowData = False

End If

End Function

3. Write the AddCamcorder function:

Public Function AddCamcorder(ByVal Product As String, _

ByVal Price As Currency, ByVal inStock As Integer, _

ByVal QtySold As Integer, _

ByVal zoom As Single) As Boolean

Dim ok As Boolean

Dim sql As String

'Build a SQL statement to insert a new

'record to the database

sql = "Insert into Camcorders" & "(Camcorder,Price,Instock,"

sql = sql &" QtySold,Zoom)" Values(" & """ & Product & """

sql = sql &"," & Price & "," & inStock

sql = sql & "," & QtySold & "," & zoom &)"

'Run the ExecuteQuery method

ok = objCon.ExecuteQuery(sql)

If ok = True Then

AddCamcorder = True

Else

AddCamcorder = False

End IfEnd Function

4. Write the fDelete function:

Public Function fDelete(ByVal RowID As Integer) As Boolean

Dim sql As String

Dim ok As Boolean

sql = "Delete From Camcorders Where RowID=" & RowID

ok = objCon.ExecuteQuery(sql)

If ok = True Then

    fDelete = True

Else

    fDelete = False

End If

End Function

5. Write the fSave function:

Public Function fSave(ByVal RowID As Integer, _

ByVal Product As String, ByVal Price As Currency, _

ByVal inStock As Integer, ByVal QtySold As Integer, _

ByVal zoom As Single) As Boolean

Dim sql As String

Dim ok As Boolean

'Build a SQL query

sql = "Update Camcorders Set"

sql = sql &" Camcorder=" & """ & Product & """

sql = sql &", Price=" & Price

sql = sql &", Instock=" & inStock

sql = sql &", QtySold=" & QtySold

sql = sql &", Zoom=" & zoom

sql = sql &" Where RowID=" & RowID

ok = objCon.ExecuteQuery(sql)

If ok = True Then

    'Signal success

    fSave = True

Else

    fSave = False

End If

End Function

c) Write the following code in the cConnector class module.

1. Write this code in the General section:

Option Explicit

Private con As ADODB.Connection

Public sCon As String

2. Write the fGetConnected function:

Private Function fGetConnected() As Boolean

Dim psCon As String

psCon = App.Path & "\Inventory.mdb"

If sCon = "" Then

sCon = psCon

End If

Set con = New ADODB.Connection

With con

.Provider = "Microsoft.Jet.OLEDB.4.0"

.ConnectionString = sCon

.Open

fGetConnected = True

End With

End Function

3. Write the ExecuteQuery function:

Public Function ExecuteQuery(ByVal sql As String) _

As Boolean

If sql = "" Then

ExecuteQuery = False

Exit Function

Else

con.Execute sql

ExecuteQuery = True

End If

End Function

4. Write the GetData function:

Public Function GetData(ByVal sqlQuery As String, _

ByRef Rs As ADODB.Recordset) As Boolean

Dim pRs As ADODB.Recordset

If sqlQuery <> "" Then

Set pRs = New ADODB.Recordset

pRs.Open sqlQuery, con, adOpenStatic, adLockReadOnly

Set Rs = pRs

GetData = True

Else

GetData = False

Exit Function

End If

End Function

In the Object drop down, select "class." This should show two events – Initialize and Terminate – in the Procedure drop down.

5. Select the Initialize event and write one line of code:

Private Sub Class_Initialize()

Call fGetConnected

End Sub

6. Select the Terminate event and write this code:

Private Sub Class_Terminate()

If con.State = adStateOpen Then

con.Close

Set con = Nothing

End If

End Sub

Congratulations! You have finished coding your class modules. Before you proceed to testing the application, it would be a very good idea to see how your newly created objects look in the Object Browser. This will also allow you to see your objects from the outside. In addition, you will be able to check if you created all object methods and properties according to the project specifications.

d) View your Objects in the Object Browser

To view your project objects in the Object Browser do the following:

Step 1. Open the project in the VB IDE (if it is not open).

Step 2. On the Toolbar click on the Object Browser button.

Step 3. In the Object Browser dialog box select *ObjectsAndClasses* project.

If you created the project according to the homework assignment, you should now be able to see four objects in the Object

Browser. These should include three class modules and one form module.

Step 4. In the Object Browser's left pane, select the cCamcorder class. This action should cause the right pane to show all methods and properties of this class.

Figure 9.2. The *ObjectsAndClasses* Project Objects.

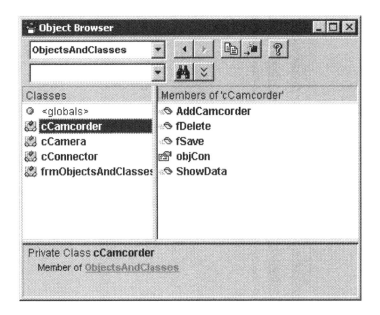

In Figure 9.2, you can see the *ObjectsAndClasses* project objects in the Object Browser. In the left pane the cCamcorder class is selected and the right pane shows all methods and properties of the class.

3. Run and Test the Application

a) Foolproof Testing

This part of testing is meant to show how your application will behave if the user does something that does not make any sense. For example, the user may click on the Add button while there are no data in the corresponding text boxes. In your program, you have written some code that is supposed to deal with potential dummy actions and now we need to check if that code works.

1.   Click on the Add, Edit, Save or Delete button while the grid is empty and the product is not selected. Do

you get a message box prompting you to select a product?

2.   Select the product from the drop down and without selecting a row in the grid try to click on the Edit or Delete buttons. What happens? Do you get a message box with the prompt: "Select a row first"?

3.   Try to add a new camera. Select the product and then type in the camera name and price and leave other text boxes empty. Click on the Add button. Do you get a message box prompting you to fill in all text boxes?

4.   Click on the Products drop down. Does the drop down list box contain two lines: Cameras and Camcorders?

5.   Select a product and then, without selecting a row in the grid, click on the Delete button. Has any row been deleted from the grid? Do you get a message box prompting you to select a row first?

6.   Click on the Close button. Does the application shut down?

If you answered "No" to any of the above questions, your program has some bugs. That's the bad news. The good news is that even if you have five "No's" it does not really mean that you have five bugs in your application. Let's now perform functionality testing. We will deal with bugs later.

b) Application Functionality Testing

1.   To test the product selection function, click on the drop down list box and select Cameras. This action should fill the grid with the Cameras data.

2.   To test the Delete button function, try to delete a
        certain item in the grid. Select a product from the
        drop down and then select any row in the grid.
        Remember the items RowID number and then click
        on the Delete button. Is that row deleted?

3.   To test the AddProduct procedure, select Cameras
        from the Products drop down, type in the data for a
        new camera and then click on the Add button. Does
        the new item immediately appear in the grid?

4.   To test the AddProduct procedure for camcorders,
        repeat test 3 to add a new camcorder.

5.   To test the EditData procedure, select any product
        and then select a row in the grid and then click on
        the Edit button. Remember the row number. Have
        that row's data been copied to the text boxes?

6.　　　　　To test the fSave function select a row, click on the Edit button, change the value of the price property in the text box beneath the "Price:" caption and click on the Save button. Does your change immediately show up in the grid?

c) Bugs Known to Dwell in this Application

If you did your testing properly, you should have noticed at least two bugs. The first bug creates a problem when the user tries to edit certain grid row data. The second allows running of the delete procedure even when the user has not selected any row in the grid. The following is a short description of each bug.

d) The Delete Button Bug

When the grid displays data but no row has been selected yet, clicking on the Delete button deletes the first row in the grid. But no delete should happen until a row is selected.

e) The Edit Button Bug

Clicking on the Edit button when the grid displays data but no row is selected does not bring up the error message box. Instead, it copies the data of the first grid row into the text boxes. However, no data copying should happen if a row is not selected.

f) How to Catch the Bugs

Please try to find the errors that feed these bugs. If you are smart enough to catch the bugs, can you find the application logic errors that cause these problems? The final task: try to fix these bugs!

In the next lesson, we will analyze the ways to fix them.

Congratulations! You have successfully completed Lesson 9.

Lesson 10

Lesson 10

Application Debugging

In this Lesson:

You will complete Project 7; you will learn how to debug your application, how to use breakpoints to stop the application execution and step into code line by line, and how to use the Immediate Window to check variable values; and you will practice breakpoint debugging technique.

Contents of Lesson 10

Part A: Create Your Homework Project

    1. Project Development, Debugging and Testing Practice

        a) Complete Project 7

        b) Application Bugs

        c) Test the Application

Part B: Application Debugging

    1. Design Time and Runtime Errors

        a) Design Time Errors

        b) Runtime Errors

    2. How to Use Breakpoints

    3. Practice Using Breakpoints

        a) Debug the AddProduct procedure

        b) How to Use the Immediate Window

    4. Learn Programming Terms

Part C: Homework Assignment Project

1. Create and Save Project 8: *ObjectsAndClassesDG*

2. Debug the Application

    a) Analysis of the Delete Button Bug

    b) The Delete Button Bug Fix

    c) Analysis of the Edit Button Bug

    d) The Edit Button Bug Fix

3. Write the Application Code

4. Run and Test the Application.

Create Your Homework Project

1. Project Development, Debugging and Testing Practice

a) Complete Project 7

Complete Project 7 according to the homework assignment described in Lesson 9. It is very important to complete this project before continuing with this lesson. When you complete the application design and coding, test the application functionality.

b) Application Bugs

There are at least two bugs in the current version of the application. The first is the delete button function bug and the second is associated with the edit button function.

c) Test the Application

Test the application functionality. Pay special attention to the Delete and the Edit buttons' functionality. Try to find out what is wrong in both functions. You will debug the application and fix errors in the next lesson.

Application Debugging

1. Design Time and Runtime Errors

Application debugging is the process of detecting and correcting the application errors. The term bug is mostly used to denote an internal logical application error. Apparently, spelling errors and typos do not qualify as bugs. We will discuss the application errors in more detail in Lesson 11; here we will briefly touch upon this topic.

a) Design Time Errors

For analysis and classification purposes, we can divide all errors into two major categories: design-time and runtime errors. In most cases, the design time errors are syntax or spelling errors. The VB compiler normally catches such errors. More importantly, the compiler does a lot of checking and verification work; it is only after all syntax, and some other errors have been corrected that the compiler compiles a program. However, the compiler is not a wizard and it cannot work magic. It cannot detect so-called internal logical errors.

b) Runtime Errors

Runtime errors are a completely different type of animal. The compiler cannot catch runtime errors for a very simple reason – these errors occur at runtime, when the program has already been compiled. All runtime errors can be divided into internal and external. The external errors are caused by external conditions. For instance, the program may be trying to read a file that has accidentally been deleted or the program may be using an invalid file path to open a file. The external errors are more or less straightforward and are relatively easy to deal with. The internal logical errors fully deserve to be called bugs because they tend to be nasty and hard to find. They get lost somewhere between hundreds and thousands of lines of code and sometimes take much more time to track down than it would take to code the whole program from scratch.

Here is a very simple example. In your program, you calculate the average sales of each salesman in ten company branches. This calculation is performed in a function procedure that uses the formula *AvrgSales = TotalSales / TotalWorkdays*. At a certain calculation point, you get the "division by zero" error. When you debug the application, you finally find out that for various reasons some salesmen has had zero workdays and you did not write any code to check that condition before you let the program run the calculation routine.

To make the programmer's life easier, VB has several tools to debug the application. The best way to help a programmer to hunt down the bugs is to allow him or her to run the application line by line and check the status of each object and variable. For this purpose, VB offers the possibility of executing the application in Debug or Break Mode. To run the application in break mode, you have to do the following: select a certain line of code and mark it as breakpoint. Then start the application. Remember the execution of code in the application will stop at the breakpoint only if a debugged procedure is in the execution scope. There is another method of putting the application into break mode – you can just use the Stop statement before the line of code where you wish to stop code execution. The beauty of break mode is not that the application code execution will stop exactly at the code line that you marked as breakpoint but in the possibility to continue to run the application line by line and check all the necessary parameters.

Thus, one of the ways to find internal logical errors is to step into code line by line and check the values of variables and/or expressions. Besides break mode and breakpoints, VB offers a number of debugging windows such as the Immediate Window, the Watch Window and the Locals Window. All these windows can also be used to monitor code execution and check the status of the application variables.

2. How to Use Breakpoints

As mentioned earlier, there are at least two big advantages of using breakpoints: First, it allows you to stop the execution of code at a desired line of code in a certain procedure. Secondly, it forces the application to run in break mode. How can you use breakpoints and break mode? Breakpoints are very useful to locate errors if you can at least estimate what procedure causes the error. Even if you have no clue where the error is located, you can still use breakpoint debugging to find the error. You can place a breakpoint at the beginning or on any particular line of code in the procedure.

So the purpose of using breakpoints is dual: to stop the application execution at a certain line of code from which you want to start the debugging, and to force the application to run in break mode. While you are stepping into code, you can check the values of any variable or expression either by moving the mouse pointer over the variable and holding it for a few seconds or by using the Immediate Window.

3. Practice Using Breakpoints

a) Debug the AddProduct procedure

Step 1. Open Project 7 in VB IDE. In the Project Explorer highlight the Form and click on the View Code button.

Step 2. Place a breakpoint by clicking on the gray margin across the AddProduct procedure's beginning wrapper line of code.

Step 3. Click on the Start button to run the application.

Step 4. Click on the Add command button. This should bring up the Code Editor window and highlight the breakpoint code line.

Step 5. Press F8 to continue execution of code line by line.

b) How to Use the Immediate Window

The Immediate Window is a very useful debugging tool. It allows you to check the value or status of any variable, expression or object in the whole project no matter if it is in execution scope or not. Of course, it will make little sense to check the value of a variable before the procedure where it is used has been executed. There is one important requirement: to use the Immediate Window you need to run your application in break mode. Note that you can bring the Immediate Window up at any time, even when the application is not running, but to get any valid application data you need to run the application in break mode.

Figure 10.1. The Immediate Window.

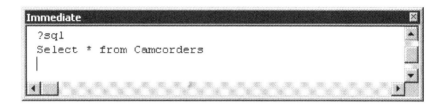

In Figure 10.1, you can see the Immediate Window showing the value of the SQL string variable in the ShowData procedure in the cCamcorder class module. To debug the application using the Immediate Window, you need to do the following:

Step 1. Run the application in break mode.

Step 2. To bring up the Immediate Window, on the View menu choose the Immediate Window.

Step 3. In the Immediate Window, type the question mark (?) and then the variable name or an expression and then press Enter. You should see the value of the variable or expression on the next line.

370

A Bug – any application logical error

Application debugging – the process of detecting and fixing the application errors

Design Time Errors – the errors that can be detected and fixed before compilation

Runtime Errors – the errors that occur when the application is running

Internal logical errors – logical or programming errors in the application code

Homework Assignment Project

Most of work in this project will focus on developing application debugging and testing skills. Please make sure that you complete all breakpoint-debugging tasks first. You should be able to detect all the bugs that we had spoken about in the previous lesson. Then start the work on fixing the bugs. There's one line of code that you should insert into each related procedure to fix the bug. After inserting that line of code, please test the application thoroughly. Check if the application works properly after the bug fix. Please remember that any typing or spelling errors may be a major source of problems or a reason why your application does not work properly.

1. **Create and Save Project 8:** *ObjectsAndClassesDG*

- In Windows Explorer, create a new folder and name it *Project8.*

- In Windows Explorer, copy frmObjectsAndClasses form and all three class modules to Project8 folder.

- Open the VB IDE and create a New Standard EXE project.

- Set the project name to *ObjectsAndClassesDG.*

- Add frmObjectsAndClasses form (it should be in Project8 folder now)

- Rename the form to frmObjectsAndClassesDG.

- Save the renamed form to Project8 folder.

- On the Project menu, choose Add Class Module. In the Add Class Module dialog box, select Existing, navigate to Project8 folder, select cCamcorder, cCamera and cConnect classes and click on the Open button.

- Remove the Form1 form.

- On the File menu, choose Save Project As; navigate to Project8 folder and save all project files in it.

2. Debug the Application

In this section, you will debug the application. Your main goal is to locate the source of errors. Please pay maximum attention to verifying the RowID variable values before and after a grid row is selected by the user.

a) Analysis of the Delete Button Bug

When the grid displays data but no row has been selected, clicking on the Delete button deletes the first row in the grid. To find the source of this error, we need to debug the cmdDelete click event procedure. Bring up the frmObjectsAndClasses form's code window. Place a breakpoint at the procedure beginning wrapper line. Run the application. Select Cameras and then, without selecting a grid row, click on the Delete button. This action should bring up the code window and highlight the first line of code in the cmdDelete click

event procedure, which should look like Listing 10.1.

Listing 10.1. The cmdDelete click event procedure.

Private Sub cmdDelete_Click()

Dim RowID As Integer

Dim DBRowID As Integer

RowID = grdInfo.RowSel

'Check if a grid row is selected

If CheckProductAndRowID <> 0 Then

Exit Sub

End If

'Read the row ID

DBRowID = grdInfo.TextMatrix(grdInfo.RowSel, 0)

Select Case cboProducts.Text

Case "Cameras"

objCameras.fDelete DBRowID

Case "Camcorders"

objCamcorders.fDelete DBRowID

End Select

Call ShowRecords

End Sub

Listing 10.2. The CheckProductAndRowID Procedure.

Private Function CheckProductAndRowID() As Integer

(1) If cboProducts.Text = "" Then

'Error: product not selected

CheckProductAndRowID = 1

MsgBox "Please select product first."

Exit Function

Else

(2) If grdInfo.RowSel = 0 Then

'Error: row not selected

CheckProductAndRowID = 3

MsgBox "Please select Row first."

Exit Function

Else

'If we get here then signal success

CheckProductAndRowID = 0

End If

End If

End Function

Now your task is to step into code line by line and check the values of variables. To step into code one line at a time, press on F8. The first line of code that will be executed will call the CheckProductAndRowID procedure, which you can find in Listing 10.2. This procedure is supposed to check both the selected product name value and the grid's selected row index. Therefore, your next press on F8 should actually take you to the CheckProductAndRowID procedure. It is in this procedure that you should find out what is wrong. In Listing 10.2, line 1 checks the cboProducts ComboBox text property value. If it is empty, the user has not selected a product yet. If the product property is not empty, we jump to the Else part of the If statement, where in line 2 we test the grid's selected row index. Here our intention is to verify if the user has selected any row or not. Since we are in break mode, we can check the row index value, either by using the Immediate Window or by using the tool tip text. To use the tool tip text method, move the mouse pointer to the grdInfo.RowSel object variable and hold it for a few seconds. The value of the RowSel property should appear as a tool tip text. If you cannot do it, try the Immediate Window. Bring up the Immediate Window and type?grdInfo.RowSel and press Enter. What is the row index value? Is it 0 or 1? You should get a value equal to 1. This is the source of our problem and we can think of only one explanation. It seems that the Microsoft Hierarchal Flex Grid control that we use in our application sets the selected row index to 1 by default. Note that the fixed row index is zero and the index of the first row that the user can select is one. Thus, we have detected the source of the problem. Let's figure out how to fix this error or rather how to create a workaround.

b) The Delete Button Bug Fix

Before we create a workaround, it will be useful to find out what kind of values can be assigned to the RowSel property. On your VB toolbar, click on the Object Browser button; in the All Libraries drop down, select MSHFlexGridLibrary; then in the left pane, select MSHFlexGrid class; then in the right pane click on the RowSel property. Now read the definition of that property. You will see that it is defined as Long Integer and that it is not available at design time. This means that it can only be set at runtime.

It would help us a lot if we could set the value of RowSel to $-$ 1, similar to the ListIndex in the ComboBox but the grid control has a restriction $-$ the row index can only be a positive number. So setting the row index to 0 is our only option. The question is when, where and how can we assign the 0 value to RowSel property? The first place where we can do it is in the form load event. In the form load event procedure, write this line of code:

380

grdInfo.RowSel = 0

Let's test the Delete button. Now it works fine.

However, what happens if we click the Delete button again after we have selected a row and deleted it but have not selected another row yet. It again deletes the first row. I click Delete once and then without selecting a row continue clicking and get rows deleted one by one. Now we have detected another bug. What happens now? We set the value of the RowSel to 0 when the form is loaded. It seems that when the grid control loses focus and then gets focus again it restores the grid's default values. Do you have any idea how to finally kill this bug? It is simple. You should reset the selected row index to 0 in each procedure that deals with it. This means that we have to set the RowSel value to 0 after each operation with the grid control.

c) Analysis of the Edit Button Bug

The Edit button bug is not only similar to the Delete button bug – it is also caused by the same condition. Clicking on the Edit button when the grid displays data but no row is selected does not bring up the message box that prompts the user to select a row; instead, it copies the data of the first row into the TextBoxes. We need to make sure that no data are copied until a row is selected.

d) The Edit Button Bug Fix

You can debug the EditData sub in the same way as you debugged the cmdDelete click event procedure. Please make sure that you comment out the fix that we created for the Delete button problem. That's because the Edit button problem has exactly the same error source. So all you have to do to fix the problem is to insert the following line of code at the end of the EditData subroutine:

grdInfo.RowSel = 0

After you have inserted this code, continue testing. Remove all break points and run the application. To remove a breakpoint, just click on the red circle. To remove all breakpoints, on the Debug menu choose Clear All Breakpoints; then select another product and now without selecting a row click on the Edit button. Does it copy the first row again or prompt you to select a row? Note that you should be able to click on the Edit button only once after a row is selected; the next click should prompt you to select a row. Did we kill all the bugs? Let's hope so.

3. Write the Application Code

To fix the bugs that we have just analyzed, you have to add the following line of code at the bottom of each related procedure:

grdInfo.RowSel = 0

Add the above line of code at the end of each of the following procedures:

Private Sub Form_Load()

Private Sub cmdDelete_Click()

Private Sub cmdSave_Click()

For example, this is how it may look in the form load event procedure:

Private Sub Form_Load()

Dim ok As Boolean

'This code will center the form

Me.Left = (Screen.Width - Me.Width) / 2

Me.Top = (Screen.Height - Me.Height) / 2

'This will add two product items to

'The ComboBox

cboProducts.AddItem "Cameras"

cboProducts.AddItem "Camcorders"

grdInfo.RowSel = 0

End Sub

4. Run and Test the Application

1. Click on the Save button on the toolbar to save your work.

2. To run your program, click on the Start button on the toolbar.

3. Check if you can run the delete function without selecting a grid row.

4. Check if you can execute the edit function when no grid row is selected.

5. Check the Add button function. Click on the Add button without selecting a product.

6. Click on the Add button when some or all text boxes are empty.

Congratulations! You have successfully completed Lesson 10.

Lesson 11

Lesson 11

Application Error Handling

In this Lesson:

Y ou will create Project 8; you will analyze and fix application bugs; and you will learn how to write code that can trap and handle runtime errors.

Contents of Lesson 11

Part A: Create Your Homework Project

 1. Project Development, Debugging and Testing Practice

Part B: Application Runtime Error Handling

 1. Error Handling

 2. Design Time Errors

 3. Internal Logical Errors

   a) Logical Errors

   b) Programming Errors

 4. How to Write Error Handlers

Part C: Homework Assignment Project

 1. Create and Save Project 9: ObjectsAndClassesEH

 2. Write Error-Handling Code

 3. Run and Test the Application

Create Your Homework Project

1. Project Development, Debugging and Testing Practice

Create Project 8 according to homework assignment in Lesson

10.

Application Runtime Error Handling

1. Error Handling

We briefly touched upon the application error types in Lesson 10. Here we would like to summarize some of the main points. We can classify all program errors with various criteria, which may include the following: the time when the error occurs, the error type, and the source of the error. From the timing standpoint, we can speak about the design time and the runtime errors. The VB compiler and auto syntax check utility help us detect most of the design time errors. When you try to compile your application, the VB compiler checks the syntax of your code in each procedure and will not compile if any error is detected. If it finds an error, it will show you an error message with the heading "Compile error" and a short description of the error.

Errors that show up when you run the application are called the runtime errors. If the source of a runtime error is in the application itself, this may be an internal logical application error. However, if the error is caused by the application environment, it is an external runtime error. External errors may be caused by a change or the absence of a certain condition in the application environment. For example, the user might have forgotten to insert a floppy disk that contains a file to be opened, or the folder that contained the file might have been deleted.

Internal runtime errors are generally called the internal logical application errors or bugs. For example, if in your application you wrote a formula or an expression in which a certain value is divided by zero, you will get a "Division by zero" runtime error. Obviously, internal logical errors cannot be detected by the VB compiler. These errors will sit like time bombs and will explode only when you try to run the application. Let's now have a closer look at design time and runtime errors.

2. Design Time Errors

What errors can occur at design time and how can we deal with them? Let's analyze a few simple examples. For instance, you type code and forget to use the parenthesis for the procedure argument list, or forget to type the "Then" keyword in your "If" statement. All these errors are detected by the Auto Syntax Check utility, which automatically checks the syntax when you type in the code. This feature is called Auto Syntax Check and it can be turned off and on from the Tools menu.

If you type the "Option Explicit" statement in the General declaration section of your module, the Code Editor will always check if all your variables are properly declared. If not, you will receive an error message saying that the identifier (variable) is not defined. Try a number of syntax errors and see what error messages the Auto Syntax Check utility will throw at you.

- Try to omit closing parentheses in a procedure argument list and you will get the error message: "Expected list separator or)"

- Try to add a few letters after the End Select statement. You should get an error message "Expected end of statement."

- Try to type any word that is not a keyword on a separate line and press Enter – you will get an error message: "Sub or Function not defined."

- Try to assign a string value to an integer type variable:

  Dim errNum as Long

  errNum = "Testing"

  You will get a "Type mismatch" error.

Pay special attention to "Type mismatch" errors. The chances are that at the beginning of your programming career you will get this error very often. You may be confused about how to interpret these errors and how to correct them. Here's what you need to do: check what type you selected when you declared the variable. Then check what value is being dynamically assigned to that variable at runtime.

In most cases, VB will do a necessary conversion for you if the underlying value allows that. For example, if you assign a value from the text box to an integer type variable, you need to make sure that the string type carried from the TextBox control is converted into integer type. For example, if the user types some numbers, VB will successfully convert them into an integer. However, if the user enters letters, VB will show you a "Type mismatch" error because it cannot convert a string into numeric type. If you want to do the conversion yourself, you may want to use the following VB built-in functions: Val(), Str() and Int(). For example, let's look how the Val() function works. If you pass a string that contains numbers, the Val() function will convert them into Double data type. If you pass a string that contains characters, the Val() function will return zero. Here's a line of code in which the Val() function is used to convert the value obtained from a TextBox into a number:

intTotalAmount = Val(Text1.Text)

What if the value typed by the user into a text box is a character string, which cannot be converted into a numeric type? To prevent such runtime errors you may need to write code that will first test what type of value it is dealing with and then decide whether to proceed or throw an error message saying that only numeric values are allowed in this field. This operation is called data validation (see Lesson 5 for more on data value testing).

3. Internal Logical Errors

To define and classify internal logical errors that may occur in your application into certain categories and classes is practically impossible and is outside the scope of this book. For discussion purposes, let's define two very diffuse categories of application internal runtime errors. The first category may be called the logical errors and the second the programming errors.

a) Logical Errors

The term logical error is self-explanatory but it may actually cover a great number of various errors. For instance, the division by zero error is a good example of a logical error because it is in fact a logical and purely mathematical error. Here's an example of code that will produce this error.

1. Type these two lines of code at the top of the ShowRecords procedure and run the application.

intNumber = 9

intValue = 0

intResult = intNumber / intValue

When you execute this code, the error will be detected by the VB runtime system one line before that line of code that attempts to divide by zero and you will get an error message saying "Run-time error 11: Division by zero."

b) Programming Errors

Programming errors could be defined as errors caused by a programmer's inattentiveness, lack of detail orientation, negligence or misunderstanding of certain programming rules and concepts. We think that the following types of errors can be included in this category, to name just a few:

- Type mismatch
- Invalid property value
- Overflow

Here are some examples and descriptions of each type.

1. The "Type mismatch" error.

One of the ways to avoid "Type mismatch" errors is always to follow a rule of two tests: first check the variable data type and then the value assigned to that variable. If you declared a variable an Integer type, you may assign only numeric values to it. So assigning a character value to an integer variable will cause a type mismatch error. Try the following: assign the "test" string value to the ListIndex property of the ComboBox:

Combo1.ListIndex = 'test"

When you run this line of code you will get a "Type mismatch" error message because the ListIndex property is defined as Long, which means that it may take only a numeric value that is within the range defined by the Long Integer data type.

2. The "Invalid property value" error.

Write code to assign -1 to the RowSel property of the grid control:

MSHFLEXGRID1.RowSel = -1

When you run this line of code, you will get an "Invalid row value" error message because the grid control's row-selected property does not allow negative values.

3. The "Overflow" error.

The overflow error may occur when you try to assign a numeric value that exceeds the range of a corresponding numeric type. For instance, the integer type is designed to hold the maximum number of 32767. If you try to assign 32678 to an Integer variable, you will get an overflow error.

4. How to Write Error Handlers

Any runtime error can halt the execution or crash your application. That's the bad news. The good news is that VB has a special mechanism to deal with runtime errors. This mechanism not only allows you to catch runtime errors but also allows you to correct error conditions and even continue program execution. This mechanism is called the VB runtime error handling. To employ this mechanism all we need to do is write error handlers in each procedure.

Error handlers can deal with expected and unexpected runtime errors. Now we will say a few words on how to understand expected and unexpected errors. If you are a smart programmer, you may think about certain situations where you can anticipate certain errors at runtime. Then you may want to write special code to deal with such expected errors. Here are a few examples of typical expected errors. Opening a connection to a database may cause an error because the network or the database may be down; opening a commonly used "ini" or XML file may cause a file open error because a file may be deleted or moved; any file open operation may cause an error if an invalid file path is used or a file is deleted; sending a document to a printer may cause an error if the printer is down or offline.

Why should you write error handlers? First, code written in your error handler allows your application to fail gracefully. This means that when the error occurs the control over the application will move to the error handler and you can inform the user about the error and provide him or her with a number of options, such as to correct the error and continue the application execution or to shut down the application. If you do not write runtime error handlers in your application, the VB runtime system will report the error and shut down the application. This situation may be defined as a case when the application failed disgracefully or simply crashed.

Writing a runtime error handler in a procedure may be divided into these steps:

Step 1. Declare variables to store the error number and the error description.

Step 2. Place the error trap line of code: *On Error Goto ErrorHandlerName*

Step 3. Write the Exit sub/function line before the error handler.

Step 4. Write the Error handler code.

Step 5. Clear the application Err object.

Before you write an error handler in any procedure, it is important to remember that the error handler in a form module will differ from an error handler written in a class module. In a class module, the error handler must pass the error that occurred in it to the application procedure that called it. Therefore, in the error handler that you write in any class module procedure you should write a line of code that raises the error and passes it to the client application. This line of code may look like this:

Raise errNumber, errDescription

Note that you do not need to raise an error when you write an error handler in a form module or a standard module procedure.

Souleiman Valiev

Listing 11.1 A sample of an error handler for a form module procedure.

Private Sub mnuAddProduct_Click()

'some code

1. On Error Goto errHandler

'some code

2. Exit Sub

3. errHandler:

4. ErrNumber = Err.Number

5. ErrDescription = Err.Description

6. Err.Clear

End Sub

Listing 11.2. A sample of an error handler in a class module procedure.

Private Sub ShowRecords()

'some code

1. ***On Error GoTo ShowRecordsErr***

   'some code

   2. Exit Sub

   3. ShowRecordsErr:

   4. errNum = Err.Number

   5. errDes = Err.Description

   6. Err.Raise errNum, "ShowRecords Procedure", errDes

End Sub

Listing 11.1 is an error handling routine written in a form module procedure. Here's a short interpretation of each line of code in this error handler. Note that line numbers are used only for discussion purposes. Line 1 is the error trap, which should be placed before any executable code in the procedure. The error trap fulfills two functions – it signals that there is an error handling routine in this procedure and points to the routine name. Line 2 instructs to exit the Sub. This line is necessary for normal execution. When no error occurs, we need to make sure that the procedure would not execute the error handling code. When an error occurs, this instruction will be ignored because the execution will go to the error handling code that starts from line 3. Lines 4 and 5 read the error number and the error description and store them in variables. Line 6 cleans the Err object to make sure that it does not store any error messages.

Listing 11.2 is the error handling routine that we have written in the ShowRecords procedure in one of our class modules. As you may notice, there is one important difference in this error handler if we compare it with the one in Listing 11.1. In Line 5, we have a code line that raises the error. This line is necessary in class module procedures because we should delegate the error that occurred in a COM server to the client application.

Homework Assignment Project

1. Create and Save Project 9: ObjectsAndClassesEH

- In Windows Explorer, create a new folder and name it *Project9.*

- In Windows Explorer, copy frmObjectsAndClassesDG and all three class modules to Project9 folder.

- Open the VB IDE and create a New Standard EXE project.

- Set the project name to *ObjectsAndClassesEH.*

- Add the frmObjectsAndClassesDG form to the project.

- Rename the frmObjectsAndClassesDG form to frmObjectsAndClassesEH.

- Save the frmObjectsAndClassesEH form to Project9.

411

- On the File menu, choose Save Project As; navigate to the Project9 folder and save the project file in it.

2. Write Error Handling Code

In this homework assignment project, you will add runtime error handlers to each procedure in the project. This will include all procedures in the form module and all procedures in three class modules.

a) In Listing 11.3, an error handler written in a form module procedure is given.

Listing 11.3. The ShowRecords form module procedure with the error handler.

Private Sub ShowRecords(ByVal iMode As Integer)

Dim rs As ADODB.Recordset

On Error goto ErrRecords

Select Case iMode

Case 1 'Cameras

Call objCameras.ShowData(rs)

Case 2 'Camcorders

Call objCamcorders.ShowData(rs)

End Select

Set grdInfo.DataSource = rs

Exit Sub

ErrRecords:

MsgBox "Error occurred: "& Err.Description &" " & Err.Number

End Sub

b) An error handler for a class module procedure.

In Listing 11.4, we have modified the ShowRecords Sub procedure to add the error handling routine.

Listing 11.4 The ShowRecords Sub with the error handler.

Souleiman Valiev

Private Sub ShowRecords()

Dim rs As ADODB.Recordset

Dim errNum As Long

Dim errDes As String

On Error GoTo ShowRecordsErr

Select Case cboProducts.Text

Case "Cameras"

Call objCameras.ShowData(rs)

Case "Camcorders"

Call objCamcorders.ShowData(rs)

End Select

Set grdInfo.DataSource = rs

Exit Sub

ShowReordsErr:

errNum = Err.Number

errDes = Err.Description

Err.Raise errNum, "ShowRecords Procedure", errDes

End Sub

1. Write the error handlers. Use the example shown in Listing 11.3 and write the runtime error handling code in the following procedures in the frmObjectsAndCalssesEH form:

AddProduct()

EditData()

ShowRecords()

CheckProductAndRowID()

2. Use the example shown in Listing 11.4 and write the runtime error handlers in the following procedures the cCamera class module:

AddCamera()

fSave()

fDelete()

ShowData()

3. Add the error handling code to the following procedures in the cCamcorder class module:

AddCamcorder()

fSave()

fDelete()

ShowData()

3. Run and Test the Application

Perform some special testing in which you should create some errors in the procedure and see how those errors are handled by the error handler.

1. In the ShowData procedure, modify the SQL query. For example, change the table name to "Cammeras."

2. Place a breakpoint at the beginning of the ShowData procedure.

3. Run the application and select a product.

Note that from line *ok = objCon.GetData(sql, pRs)* the execution will go to the class module function GetData(), where it will cause an error when it tries to open the recordset. The error will be caused by a misspelled table name in the SQL statement. Now that the class module function has the error handler in place, the error will be caught there. If there were no error handler in that function, the error would have been returned to the ShowData procedure. Thus, the role of an error handler is to signal that there is an error handler in the procedure and to deal with the error condition. The application stores its errors in the Err object and then looks for the error handling code in the procedure where the error occurred. If it finds one, it runs the code that you have written in the error handler. In the error handler routine, you can handle the error situation in various ways. For example, you may:

a) Show a default message box with the OK button.

b) Show a custom message box with Continue and Close buttons.

c) Log the error number and description and shut down the application.

If you decide to continue application execution, you need to consider the possibility of other procedures failing if they depend on the data processed by the failed procedure or by the procedure that caused the error.

4. Test all functions after you have inserted the error handlers.

Congratulations! You have successfully completed Lesson 11.

Lesson 12

Lesson 12

How to Create Menus and

Open Files

In this Lesson:

You will create Project 9; you will learn how to design menus; you will create menu click event procedures; you will learn how to program file open, file read and file write procedures and how to debug file manipulation statements.

Contents of Lesson 12

Part A: Create Your Homework Project

   1. Project Development, Debugging and Testing Practice

Part B: How to Create Menus and Open Files

   1. How to Create Menus

   2. How to Programmatically Open Files

      a) File Open Methods

      b) Writing a File Open Statement

   3. How to Programmatically Read from a File

   4. How to Programmatically Write to a File

   5. File Open Error Handling

   6. Learn Computer Guru Jargon

Part C: Homework Assignment Project

   1. Create and Save Project 10: Menus

   2. Redesign the frmMenus Form

a) Remove TextBoxes, Labels and CommandButtons

b) Create Menus

3. Add Controls and Set their Properties

4. Write the Application Code

5. Run and Test the Application

Create Your Homework Project

1. Project Development, Debugging and Testing Practice

Create Project 9 according to the homework assignment in Lesson 11. It is very important to complete this project before continuing with this lesson.

How to Create Menus and Open Files

1. Creating Menus

Using menus in an application saves a lot of space on the form and makes a user interface look and function more efficiently. Creating menus in your application is simplified by VB. All you need to know is how to create the top menu item; then you can create the child menu items that will be displayed beneath the parent menu; and finally you will learn how to write code that will be executed whenever the user clicks on the menu.

To create a menu in your application, you should use the Menu Editor. In the Menu Editor, you have to type the menu caption and the menu programmatic name and click on the OK button. The

427

menu caption will be used as the menu's title, while the menu's

programmatic name will serve as the menu object identifier in code.

Figure 12.1 The Menu Editor.

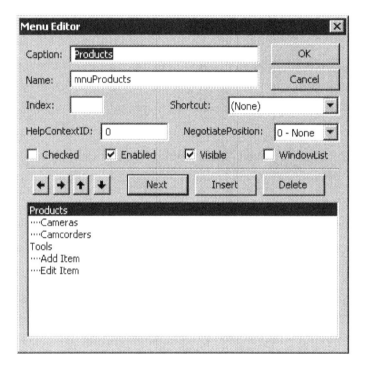

In Figure 12.1, the Menu Editor is shown. Note that the Menu

Editor button on the Toolbar is disabled if the form is not displayed in

the VB IDE. Therefore, before you start working on menus, you need to bring up the form object. Let's break down the menu creation process into three steps.

Step 1: Creating the parent menu. This menu will appear in the menu bar on the form.

Create the Menu Title

- To bring up the Menu Editor, click on the Menu Editor button on the toolbar.
- Type the caption of the menu in the Caption text box.

Create the Menu Name

- In the Name text box, type in the menu's programmatic name.

You may want to add the "mnu" prefix before the name to remind you that it is a menu object. For example, you may create the mnuProducts menu.

- Click on the Next button to move to the next line.

Step 2: Creating child menus. These menus will appear under the parent menu.

- Type the menu caption and programmatic name.
- Click on the right-pointing arrow to make this item a child menu.
- Click on the Next button if you want to create another menu. Otherwise, click on the OK button.

Step 3: Writing code in the menu click event procedure.

Writing code for each menu click event procedure is the most important part of the work. You may write all the necessary code in the menu click event procedure or you may write code in separate procedures and then call them. The goal is to implement all the functionality implied by the menu title. For example, if you are going to create a File menu with such common submenus as Open, Close and Save, the code written for those menus should provide all the expected functionality. If you want to write all the necessary code in the menu click event procedure, you need to do the following:

- Bring up the form's code editor window.
- From the Object drop down, select the necessary menu object.

This will bring up the code editor and show the click event subroutine for that menu. For example, in our project the mnuCameras menu click event sub looks like this:

Private Sub mnuCameras_Click()

productID = "cameras"

Call ShowRecords(1)

End Sub

In the *mnuCameras* click event procedure there are two lines of code. In the first line, we assign a value to the product ID variable

431

to specify the product category. In the second line, we call the ShowRecords subroutine procedure that will display the data. Thus, the code that we have written in this procedure is used to display the product data that belong to a selected product category.

2. How to Programmatically Open Files

All physical files differ in their type of record access. There are sequential access and random access files. In random access files, records are accessed record by record; in sequential files, records are accessed line by line. In sequential files, each line is a text line. In this section, we will discuss how to programmatically manipulate sequential files.

In your application, you may need to programmatically open, read or write to a certain physical file. The term programmatically is used here to emphasize that the file will be opened and manipulated by your program's code. This can be done using a set of built-in VB functions, such as Open(), Close(), Input(), and Write(). To implement the file manipulation functionality, you need a file path and you have to write code that will actually open a file and read or write to it.

a) File Open Methods

What you can do with a file depends on how you open it. Sequential files can be opened in one of these three ways: For Input, For Output and For Append.

For Input

Files opened For Input are meant for reading the data, so they allow read-only access.

For Output

Files opened For Output are meant to write to them. If the file does not exist, it will be created. However, if the file exists it will be deleted and then created anew. If you provide a valid file path, the file will be created in that directory. Note that if you pass a zero-length string as a file path, the file will be created in the application directory by default. Normally the application directory is the directory where the application executable file is located. If you are in design mode, the application directory is the directory where your project file is located. After the file is created, you may use the Write or Print command to add text lines to the file.

For Append

If you need to add records to an existing file, the best way to do it is to open the file For Append. Note that For Append is similar to For Output with one important exception – that if the file exists it will not be deleted.

The File Path

The file path may be hard-coded in the program or it may be obtained dynamically when the program is running. The file path must include the following parts: the disk name or letter, the path to the folder that contains the file and the file name with the file name extension.

For example: D:\Projects\VBProjects\Controls.vbp

b) How to Write a File Open Statement

To programmatically open a file, you need to obtain the file path and then obtain a free file number. To get a free file number, use the FreeFile() function. Then write the file open statement. This should include the following elements: the Open keyword, a file path, the access type keyword, and the file number proceeded by a "#". Let's break this process down into the following steps:

Step 1: Get the file path.

Create a string variable and assign the file path value to it:

Dim strFilePath as String

strFilePath = "c:\DataFiles\Products.txt"

Step 2: Get a free file number.

Create a Long type variable and assign a free file number to it:

435

Dim lngFileNumber as Long

lngFileNumber = FreeFile()

Step 3: Build a file open statement.

Open strFilepath For Input As #lngFileNumber

Step 4: Close the file.

Close #lngFileNumber

When we are done with the file, we need to close it. Use the Close() function plus the file number to close a file. Note that if you run the Close statement without specifying the file number, all open files will be closed.

3. How to Programmatically Read from a File

Once a file is open, you may use it either to read the content of the file or to write to it. There are several ways you can read the content of a file. You may extract the entire content of the file, you may get just one line, or you may read one byte at a time. This will depend on how you opened the file and what function you use in the file read statement. Let's break this operation down into two steps:

Step 1: Write the file open statement. Your file open statement may look like this:

Open FileName For Input as #FileNum

Step 2: Write the read file content statement. Create a variable that will store the file content and then execute a file read statement that may use the Input() function. Your code may look like this:

437

Dim strFileContent as String

str*FileContent = Input(FileLen(Filename), #FileNum)*

In step 2, we have declared a string type variable and then assigned the content of the file to it. Note that the Input() function takes the following arguments: the length of the content to be extracted from the file, and the opened file number. The length parameter allows you to extract any number of characters from the file. For example, the above statement will extract the entire content of the file into the *strFileContent* variable because we set the length parameter to the full size of the file. Once you have extracted the content, you may use it in code.

4. How to Programmatically Write to a File

To write to a file, you need to create the file and then write the necessary content to it. There are two ways to write to a file: you may write or write to append. In other words, you may write certain information to a file or you may add a piece of information to an existing file. To do the first, you need to open the file For Output. To add records to an existing file, you have to open the file For Append. As mentioned earlier, what you can do with a file largely depends on how you open it. Remember that if you open one of the existing files For Output, the content of the file will be erased and the file will be recreated. If you open an existing file For Append, its content will be preserved and new records may be added to it. You can accomplish a write to a file operation in two steps:

Step 1: Write a file open statement:

Dim lngFileNumber as Long

Dim strFilePath as String

Dim strContent as String

lngFileNumber = FreeFile()

strFilePath = "c:\MyFiles\Products.txt"

'Open a file to write:

Open strFilePath For Output As #lngFileNumber

Step 2: Build a write statement:

strContent = "This is a text line."

Write #lngFileNumber, strContent

Close #lngFileNumber

Note that in step 2 we assign a text to a string variable; then we use the Write() function to write the content of the variable to the file. In the third line of code, we close the file.

5. File Open Error Handling

There is at least one file open runtime error that you should avoid at any cost. This is the "File not found" error. If such an error occurs in your application and it is not handled properly, you will get a "File not found" VB runtime error.

a) File not Found Runtime Error

If a file path variable passed to the file open statement contains a zero-length string, you will get the following file path error:

Run-Time Error 75: "Path/File Access Error"

If the file path variable is not empty but carries an invalid file path, you will get a "File not found" runtime error:

Run-time Error 53: "File not found"

It is a good programming practice to take special precautions to avoid these errors. Actually, the probability of these and some other file manipulation errors can be reduced to zero if you do a few tests before you execute a file open or a file read statement. The following

441

two tests are enough to prevent execution of an invalid file open statement.

Test 1: Test the file path expression

You may use the file path expression directly as a parameter in your file open statement or you may store it in a variable and then use that variable in the file open statement. If you do not use a variable to store the file path expression, you may skip this test or perform only the syntax check part of this test. However, we would recommend that you always use a variable to store the file path. Remember you may hard-code the file path expression in your application variable or obtain it dynamically and then assign it to a variable.

The depth of the file path expression test will depend on how strict your error tolerance requirements are. In fact, you can perform a few subtests within this test. The first and perhaps the most important test should check whether the variable contains a value or is empty. The second subtest is designed to find out if the value is a string or a numeric type. We assume that the file path expression should be a string that may contain alphanumeric data. The third subtest may be designed to check the syntax of the file path expression. Therefore, we can divide this test into two steps: the valid data test, and the syntax test.

The Valid Data Test

The essence of this test is to find out if the variable that is used to store the file path contains any valid alphanumeric data. You can use any method to check the value of a variable. You can use the If statement and (<> "") not equal to zero-length string expression:

If strFilePath <> " " Then

   'some code

End if

The Syntax Test

The goal of this test is to check the file path expression syntax. There are at least two syntax elements that you might want to check in the file path expression: the colon (:) and the backward slash (\) if you assume that the file resides on a local computer. To test if the file path expression contains these two characters you may use the InStr() function. The InStr() function takes four arguments and returns an integer that indicates the position of the searched character in the searched expression. The first argument is a start position, the second is the searched expression and the third is the expression to search for, which can be one or more characters. If the searched character or characters are not found, the InStr(0 function will return zero. Your code that searches for colon (:) and (\) may look like this:

intVar = InStr(StartPosition, strExpression, ":")

intVar = InStr(StartPosition, strExpression, "\")

If the searched character is found in the expression, the InStr() function should return a value greater than zero. However, if the

InStr() function returns zero, the expression does not contain the searched character.

Test 2: Check if a file exists

This test is more file specific. There may be situations when you have a correct file path that points to a non-existent file. Thus, this test will check if the file exists before attempting to open it. In this test you may use the Dir() function to verify if a certain file exists in a certain directory. The Dir() function accepts the file path parameter and returns the file name if the file exists. If the file does not exist, it returns a zero-length string. You may use this test in the *If* statement and execute the file open statement only if the file exists test is successful. Your code may look like this:

If Dir(strFilePath) <> "" Then

'File open statement goes here

End if

Using both tests will allow you to eliminate the possibility of file open statement error.

Note that you can use a set of built-in VB file manipulation functions that belong to the FileSystem library. The Dir() function is one of them. However, there is a more elaborate set of file manipulation functions that belong to the Microsoft Scripting Runtime library. To use these functions you need to create a FileSystemObject object.

b) End of File (EOF) Error

In some cases, you may need to read only a part of the file content. Let's say you need to read only one line of text or several lines or characters. Therefore, if you read a file and need to extract one line at a time or a certain number of characters per each input statement, you need to check the end of file property each time before you execute the next input statement. If you ignore the end of file test, you may get the end of file runtime error:

Run-time error 62: "Input past end of file"

This error may be caused by the following conditions:

- You have extracted all data from this file and reached the end of the file.
- Your Input statement is trying to read an empty file.
- You have tried to test a file opened for binary access for the EOF condition.

How To Avoid this Error

Use the EOF() function immediately before the Input statement to detect the end of file condition. If the file is opened for binary access, use Seek and Loc.

Listing 12.1. Use of the EOF() function in the file read loop.

Open strFilePath For Input As #lngFileNum

For i = 0 To 7

If Not EOF(lngFileNum) Then

s = s & Input(3, #lngFileNum)

Else

Exit For

End If

Next

Close #lngFileNum

In Listing 12.1, we have a For Next loop that iterates 8 times to read the content of the file and extract 3 characters in each iteration. To avoid the EOF error, we used the EOF() function to test the end of file condition before the input statement was executed.

To massage data – to process data

A box – a computer

A black box – a code component or program without the source code

A white box – a code component or program with the source code

To recycle a box – to restart a computer

To recycle the IIS - to restart the Internet Information Server program

The Oracle box – a computer that runs Oracle database

The MSMQ box – a computer that runs MSMQ server program

A process – a program

A utility – a program or a function that may perform services

A routine – a procedure in an application

- In Windows Explorer, create a new folder and name it *Project10.*

- In Windows Explorer, copy the frmObjectsAndClassesEH form and all three classes from Project9 folder to Project10 folder.

- Open the VB IDE and create a New Standard EXE project.

- Set the project name to *Menus.*

- Add the frmObjectsAndClassesEH from Project10 folder.

- Rename the frmObjectsAndClassesEH form to *frmMenus.*

- Save the renamed form in Project10 folder.

- Rename the Form1 form to frmData.

- On the File menu choose Save Project As; navigate to Project10 folder and save the project file in it.

2. Redesign the frmMenus Form

a) Remove TextBoxes, Labels and CommandButtons.

Your modification of the frmMenus form will consist of two major parts: removing some controls and creating menus. Remove TextBoxes, Labels and CommandButtons that were used to add, save or edit data. On the redesigned form, you should have the following controls: two CommandButtons – Delete and Close; one hierarchal flex grid control; and two menus.

b) Create Menus

To start working on menus, bring up the frmMenus form and click on the Menu Editor button on the Toolbar.

Create the Products menu.

In the Caption text box, type "Products".

In the Name text box, type "mnuProducts" and click on the Next button.

To make the next menu a child menu, click on the right-pointing arrow.

In the Caption text box, type "Cameras".

In the Name text box, type "mnuCameras" and click on the Next button.

In the Caption text box, type "Camcorders".

In the Name text box, type "mnuCamcorders" and click on the Next button.

Create the Tools menu.

Click on the left-pointing arrow to move the cursor to the initial position.

In the Caption text box, type "Tools".

In the Name text box, type "mnuTools" and click on the Next button.

To make a child menu, click on the right-pointing arrow.

In the Caption text box type "Add Item".

In the Name text box type "mnuAdd" and click on the Next button.

In the Caption text box type "Edit Item".

In the Name text box type "mnuEdit" and click on the OK button.

When you finish form redesign, your completed form should look like the one shown in Figure 12.2

Figure 12.2. The frmMenus form.

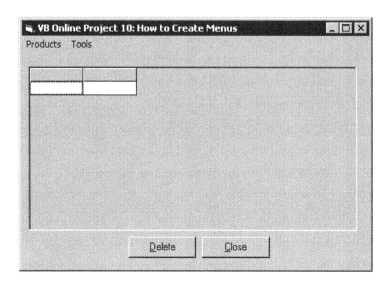

3. Add Controls and Set their Properties

Add controls to the frmData form and set their properties according to Table 12.1.

Table 12.1. The frmData form controls.

Control	Property	Value
Label	Caption	Product Name
Label	Caption	Price
Label	Caption	In Stock
Label	Caption	Qty Sold
Label	Caption	Zoom/Res
TextBox	Name	txtProductname
TextBox	Name	txtPrice
TextBox	Name	txtInStock
TextBox	Name	txtQtySold
TextBox	Name	txtZoom
CommandButton	Name	cmdSave
CommandButton	Name	cmdClose

When you complete the frmData form design, your form should look like the one shown in Figure 12.3

Figure 12.3 The frmData form.

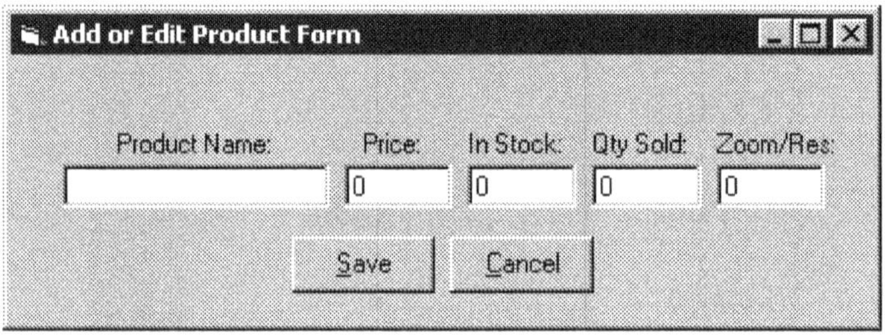

4. Write the Application Code.

1. Declare module level variables.

In the frmMenus form General section, declare module level variables and constants. Why do we need to use constants? In this application, we have declared a number of integer type constants. Although these constants hold integer values, they have string names, which make them much more meaningful and readable than just numbers. Then we created a module level integer variable iProduct and assigned the constants to this variable. Pay attention to how we use constants in the CheckProductRowID, AddProduct and EditData procedures.

In the General section, declare a module level variable iProduct. This variable will be used to keep track of the current product selection made by the user. In the Form Load event, set this variable's value to 0:

Option Explicit

Private objCameras As New cCamera

Private objCamcorders As New cCamcorder

Private iProduct As Integer

Private Const CAMERA As Integer = 5

Private Const CAMCORDER As Integer = 6

Private Const ROWSELECTED As Integer = 2

Private Const PRODUCTSEL As Integer = 1

2. Remove the following controls from the frmMenus form:

cboProducts, cmdAdd, cmdSave, cmdEdit.

3. Delete code associated with the removed controls. In the form module code editor select General in the Object drop down list box. Find and delete the following procedures:

cboProducts_click()

cmdAdd_click()

cmdSave_Click()

cmdEdit_Click()

4. Modify the CheckPrioductAndRowID function. Name it CheckProductRowID.

This function will return four different values. Two of them are the integer constants PRODUCTSEL and ROWECTED. We are going to use these two constants in procedures that invoke this function. We have created two methods to deal with the frmData form when we need to send data to the frmData form and receive edited or new data back from it. The first method may be called a direct reading from frmData. In this case we show frmData, let the user fill in the text boxes and then hide the form. Then from the frmMenus form we read the frmData text boxes values. The second method uses a special function fStart written in the frmData form. This function is used as a carrier of data from the frmMenus form to the frmData form and back. It will use the ByRef parameters to pass empty variables that will be filled in the frmData form and returned back to the calling procedure. In both methods, we need to take special care when the user wants to cancel the operation and decides to shut down the form.

5. Write the AddProduct Sub

Note that in the AddProduct Sub we use a direct method to get data from the frmData form.

Souleiman Valiev

Private Sub AddProduct()

Dim ok As Boolean

Dim Product As String

Dim inStock As Integer

Dim Price As Currency

Dim QtySold As Integer

Dim zoom As Single

If CheckProductRowID(1) <> PRODUCTSEL Then

Exit Sub

End if

frmData.CleanUp

frmData.Show 1

'Check what button was clicked

'This value is stored in the UserClosedForm

If frmData.UserClosedForm = True Then Exit Sub

'Check if the text boxes are filled

'And then read the data

460

With frmData

If .txtProductName <> "" Then Product = .txtProductName

If .txtPrice <> "" Then Price = .txtPrice

If .txtInstock <> "" Then inStock = .txtInstock

If .txtQtySold <> "" Then QtySold = .txtQtySold

If .txtZoom <> "" Then zoom = .txtZoom

End With

'Check again if each variable has value.

If Product <> "" And Price <> 0 And inStock <> 0 _

And QtySold <> 0 And zoom <> 0 Then

Select Case iProduct

Case CAMERA

ok = objCameras.AddCamera(Product, _

Price, inStock, QtySold, zoom)

Case CAMCORDER

ok = objCamcorders.AddCamcorder(Product, _

Price, inStock, QtySold, zoom)

End Select

Call ShowRecords

Souleiman Valiev

Else

'If we get here then some text boxes are empty

MsgBox "Fill in all text boxes and try again."

End If

End Sub

6. Call the AddProduct sub from the mnuAdd click event procedure.

Private Sub mnuAdd_Click()

    Call AddProduct

End Sub

7. Write the EditData sub. In this Sub, we use the fStart function to communicate with the frmData form module.

Private Sub EditData()

Dim selectedRow As Integer

Dim Product As String

Dim inStock As Integer

Dim Price As Currency

Dim QtySold As Integer

Dim zoom As Single

Dim dbRecordID As Integer

Dim ok As Boolean

'if product or row is not selected we are out of here

If CheckProductRowID(2) <> ROWSELECTED Then

Exit Sub

End if

'Find out which grid row is selected

selectedRow = grdInfo.RowSel

' Move to the user selected row

grdInfo.Row = selectedRow

'Get the record id

dbRecordID = grdInfo.TextMatrix(selectedRow, 0)

'Now we'll read column values

'and store them in variables

Product = grdInfo.TextMatrix(selectedRow, 1)

Souleiman Valiev

Price = grdInfo.TextMatrix(selectedRow, 2)

inStock = grdInfo.TextMatrix(selectedRow, 3)

QtySold = grdInfo.TextMatrix(selectedRow, 4)

zoom = grdInfo.TextMatrix(selectedRow, 5)

If frmData.fStart(1, Product, inStock, Price, _

QtySold, zoom) Then

'We assume that the values are edited

Select Case iProduct

Case CAMERA

ok = objCameras.fSave(dbRecordID, Product, _

Price, inStock, QtySold,zoom)

Case CAMCORDER

ok = objCamcorders.fSave(dbRecordID, _

Product, Price, inStock, QtySold, zoom)

End Select

End If

Call ShowRecords

grdInfo.RowSel = 0

End Sub

8. Call the EditData sub from the mnuEdit click event procedure.

Private Sub mnuEdit_Click()

Call EditData

End Sub

9. Write the CheckProductRowID function.

Private Function CheckProductRowID(ByVal iMode _

As Integer) As Integer

Select Case iMode

Case 1 'product only

If iProduct <> 0 Then

CheckProductRowID = PRODUCTSEL

Else

'Product is not selected

CheckProductRowID = 4

MsgBox "Select product first."

End If

Case 2 'both

If iProduct <> 0 Then

CheckProductRowID = PRODUCTSEL

If grdInfo.RowSel > 0 Then

'success

CheckProductRowID = ROWSELECTED

Else

' Row is not selected

CheckProductRowID = 3

MsgBox "Please select a row."

End If

Else

'Product is not selected

CheckProductRowID = 4

MsgBox "Select product first."

End If

End Select

End Function

10. Write the ShowRecords sub that will retrieve data and show it in the grid control.

Private Sub ShowRecords()

Dim rs As ADODB.Recordset

Select Case iProduct

Case CAMERA

Call objCameras.ShowData(rs)

Case CAMCORDER

Call objCamcorders.ShowData(rs)

End Select

Set grdInfo.DataSource = rs

End Sub

11. Call the ShowRecords sub from the mnuCameras click and the mnuCamcorder click event procedures:

Private Sub mnuCamcorders_Click()

iProduct = CAMCORDER

Call ShowRecords

End Sub

Private Sub mnuCameras_Click()

iProduct = CAMERA

Call ShowRecords

End Sub

12. In the cmdDelete click event procedure write code that will delete a selected record in the database:

Private Sub cmdDelete_Click()

Dim RowID As Integer

'Check if any grid row was selected

If CheckProductRowID(2) <> ROWSELECTED Then

Exit Sub

End if

RowID = grdInfo.TextMatrix(grdInfo.RowSel, 0)

'Determines which row to delete

Select Case iProduct

Case CAMERA

objCameras.fDelete RowID

Case CAMCORDER

objCamcorders.fDelete RowID

End Select

Call ShowRecords

grdInfo.RowSel = 0

End Sub

Private Sub Form_Load()

    Dim ok As Boolean

    'This code will center the form

    Me.Left = (Screen.Width - Me.Width) / 2

    Me.Top = (Screen.Height - Me.Height) / 2

    grdInfo.RowSel = 0

    iProduct = 0

End Sub

Souleiman Valiev

13. From the cmdClose click event procedure call the Unload method to close the form:

Private Sub cmdClose_Click()

Unload frmMenus

End Sub

14. Write Code in the frmData form module.

Option Explicit

Public UserClosedForm As Boolean

The fStart function will be called from the frmMenus form:

Public Function fStart(ByVal iMode As Integer, _

ByRef Product As String, _

ByRef inStock As Integer, ByRef Price As Currency, _

ByRef QtySold As Integer, ByRef zoom As Single) As Boolean

If iMode <> 0 Then

Select Case iMode

470

Case 1 'Edit mode

txtProductName.Text = Product

txtInstock.Text = inStock

txtPrice.Text = Price

txtQtySold.Text = QtySold

txtZoom.Text = zoom

Me.Show 1

Case 2 'Add product mode

txtProductName.Text = ""

txtInstock.Text = ""

txtPrice.Text = ""

txtQtySold.Text = ""

txtZoom.Text = ""

Me.Show 1

End Select

'Check the user action which is stored in

'the UserClosedForm variable. If it is true

'we should exit this function.

If UserClosedForm = True Then Exit Function

Product = txtProductName.Text

inStock = txtInstock.Text

Price = txtPrice.Text

QtySold = txtQtySold.Text

zoom = txtZoom.Text

fStart = True

Else

fStart = False

End If

End Function

Public Sub CleanUp()

    txtProductName.Text = ""

    txtPrice.Text = ""

    txtInstock.Text = ""

    txtQtySold.Text = ""

    txtZoom.Text = ""

End Sub

When the user clicks on the Cancel button, we will set the UserClosedForm variable to True and close the form:

Private Sub cmdCancel_Click()

UserClosedForm = True

Unload Me

End Sub

When the user clicks on the Save button, all we need to do is to validate data input and close the form:

Private Sub cmdSave_Click()

Dim Product As String

Dim inStock As Integer

Dim Price As Currency

Dim QtySold As Integer

Dim zoom As Single

'We use this procedure to validate user input

'if all textboxes are filled hide the form

'If any text box is empty then

Souleiman Valiev

```
'show a message box and keep the form displayed

If txtProductName <> "" And txtPrice <> "" _

And txtInstock <> "" And txtQtySold <> "" _

And txtZoom <> "" Then

Me.Hide

Else

MsgBox "Please fill in all text boxes."

End If

End Sub


Private Sub Form_Load()

        Me.Left = (Screen.Width - Me.Width) / 2

        Me.Top = (Screen.Height - Me.Height) / 2

        UserClosedForm = False

End Sub


Private Sub Form_Unload(Cancel As Integer)

        UserClosedForm = True

End Sub
```

5. Run and Test the Application

Figure 12.4 The frmMenus form at runtime.

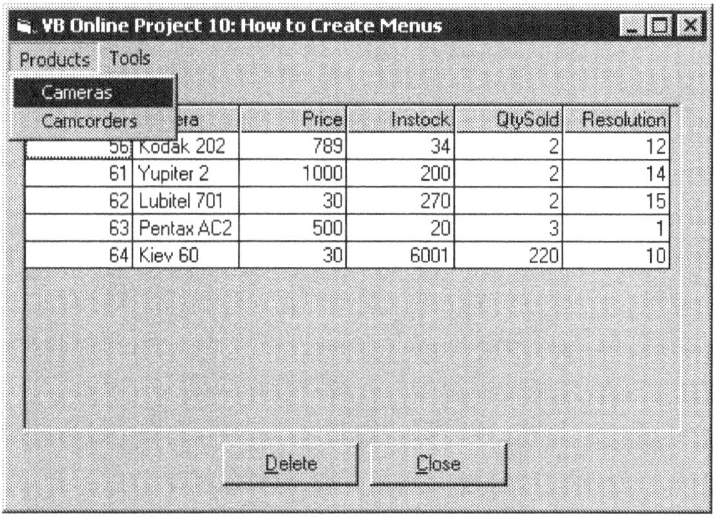
VB Online Project 10: How to Create Menus
Products
Tools
Cameras
Camcorders
Price
Instock
QtySold
Resolution
56 Kodak 202 789 34 2 12
61 Yupiter 2 1000 200 2 14
62 Lubitel 701 30 270 2 15
63 Pentax AC2 500 20 3 1
64 Kiev 60 30 6001 220 10
Delete
Close

1. Start the application. Click on the Products menu and select Cameras. Does the grid control show the Cameras data? Your form should display data as shown in Figure 12.4. Repeat this test with Camcorders.

2.   With one of the products selected and the corresponding data displayed in the grid, try to add a new record to the Cameras table. Does the frmData form pop up with the empty text boxes? If it does, fill in the text boxes and click on the Save button. The frmData form should disappear. Does the new record appear in the grid?

3.   With one of the products selected, try to edit data in any row. Click on the row in the grid. On the Tools menu choose Edit. The frmData form should pop up. Does it contain a copy of the data from the selected grid row? If it does, edit the data in one or two text boxes and then click on the Save button. Do all the changes appear in the grid? If you answered yes to all questions, you have successfully created and tested your application.

Congratulations! You have completed Lesson 12.

Lesson 13

Lesson 13

How to Use the Sub Main and

a Login Form

In this lesson:

Y ou will create Project 10; you will learn how to use the Sub Main as a project startup object, learn how to program the login form to provide the user authentication, and learn how to use the MsgBox() function to display a message and get the user response.

Contents of Lesson 13

Part A: Create Your Homework Project

1. Project Development, Debugging and Testing Practice

Part B: How to Use the Sub Main and a Login Form

1. The Sub Main as a Program Startup Object

2. How to Create a Login Form

3. How to Program the MsgBox Function

      a) The MsgBox Function Arguments

      b) How to Use the MsgBox Function's Return Value

4. How to Compile an Application

Part C: Homework Assignment Project

1. Create and Save Project 11: *LoginProject*

2. Add Controls and Set their Properties

3. Write the Application Code

4. Run and Test the Application

5. Compile your Project

6. Extra Credit Tasks

Create Your Homework Project

1. Project Development, Debugging and Testing Practice

Create Project 10 according to the homework assignment described in Lesson 12. It is very important to complete this project before continuing with this lesson.

How to Use the Sub Main and a Login Form

1. The Sub Main as a Program Startup Object

The Sub Main should be created in a standard module and it must be declared Public to make it globally visible. The Sub Main will function as an entry point to your application and any arguments passed to it may be used as the application's command line parameters. One of the main reasons for using the Sub Main in an application is wanting an object other than a form to fulfill the role of a dispatcher that starts and then controls the execution process. Here is how the Sub Main procedure may look:

Public Sub Main()

      'some code

485

End Sub

Note that the Form object and the Sub Main are the only two objects that can perform the role of an application startup object. The mission of the Sub Main may vary and largely depends on the type of application. For instance, you may use the Sub Main to control the user login and the authentication process before you allow the user to access the program's main interface; to make decisions and set privileges, limit the number of login attempts, allow access to certain functionality, prompt to change a password and so on.

Here is what we need to do to authenticate the user before we allow access to the program. Note that in this process, we will use the Sub Main, the Login form, and the MsgBox() function. From the Sub Main procedure, we will display the Login form, obtain the user input, authenticate the user and then make a decision to allow or deny access to the application. During this process, we will communicate with the user by displaying message boxes from the Sub Main procedure until we finally make a decision to display the program's main user interface to shut down the application.

2. How to Create a Login Form

Use a new form module to create a Login form. Add two labels, two TextBoxes and two CommandButtons. Your completed form should look like the one shown in Figure 13.1.

Figure 13.1 The frmLogin Form.

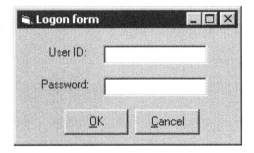

We will write the authentication code in a separate procedure that will be called from the OK button click event procedure. If the

487

authentication procedure returns false, we inform the user that either the user name or the password is invalid and allow him to try again by displaying the empty login form. When the authentication procedure returns true, we will show the application's main window. If the user clicks on the Cancel button, we will shut down the application.

3. How to Program the MsgBox Function

Up to now, we have used the MsgBox() function just to display messages to the user. This use of the function does not allow us to get the user's response. Nor will it allow the user to indicate his reaction to the information displayed in the message box. However, in this situation the user's response is crucially important. To get the user's response, we need to configure the MsgBox() function to show a desired set of buttons and to return a value that reflects the user's decision. By using the MsgBox() function in this way, we will achieve the following goals: display a necessary message, display a set of buttons, and obtain a return value that will indicate which button was clicked. Thus, we will be able to communicate a message to a user and get a response. In the next section you will learn how to program the MsgBox() function.

a) The MsgBox Function Arguments

The MsgBox() function is one of the VB built-in functions that can do the following:

1. Display a message.
2. Display an icon that distinguishes the type of the message box.
3. Display a set of buttons.
4. Display a message box title.
5. Display context sensitive help.
6. Return a value that identifies which button was pressed by the user.

The MsgBox() function accepts the following arguments:

1. Prompt (the text of the message).

2. Buttons (the Message box Icon indicator + Buttons Indicator).

3. Title (the message box title).

4. HelpFile (the help file).

5. Context (the help context indicator).

Thus, the MsgBox() function accepts five arguments. The first argument is required while all others are optional. Note that if you do not pass optional arguments the default values will be used. Here's the description of each argument:

Prompt

The Prompt argument is required. It accepts a text string, which will be displayed in the message box.

Buttons

The Buttons argument is used to specify what buttons you would like to display on the message box. The following constants may be used as button settings parameters:

VbYesNo – will display the Yes and No buttons.

VbOKCancel – will display the OK and Cancel buttons.

VbRetryCancel – will display the Retry and Cancel buttons.

VbNoYesCancel – will display the No, Yes and Cancel buttons.

VbAbortRetryIgnore – will display the Abort, Retry and Ignore buttons.

VbOKOnly – will display the OK button only.

The MsgBox() function can display four types of message boxes. The only thing that makes these message boxes look different is the icon displayed in the top left-hand corner. To set the type of icon, you may use the following constants:

vbCritical, vbExclamation, vbError and vbInformation.

Note that the Buttons argument is used to specify both a set of buttons to display and the icon type. So to specify both the icon type and the buttons you have to use both constants connected by a plus sign:

vbCritical + vbOKCancel

Title

The Title argument is used to set the title of the message box. Note that if you do not pass the title parameter, the project name will be used by default.

Examples:

Example 1: The following code will display the message box shown in Figure 13.2:

MsgBox "Enter User ID."

Figure 13.2. The OK message box.

Note that if you do not provide any of the optional arguments the default values will be used. For example in Figure 13.2, the project name is used as the title because we did not provide the title parameter.

Example 2: The following code will display a message box shown in Figure 13.3:

MsgBox "Invalid User ID. Try again?", vbCritical + VbRetryCancel

Figure 13.3. The Retry and Cancel message box.

Example 3: The following code will display the message box

shown in Figure 13.4:

MsgBox "Connection failed. Try again?", vbExclamation +

vbYesNoCancel, "Connection status"

Figure 13.4. The Yes/No/Cancel message box.

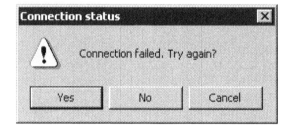

b) How to Use the MsgBox() Function's Return Value

To use the MsgBox() function's return value, you need to assign the return value to an Integer type variable and then use the variable in code. To interpret the returned value, we can use either the VB constants or the direct numeric values to identify which button was pressed on the message box. Of course, using the constants make this task much easier. With the constants, the interpretation technique is simple: you need to compare the return value with a certain constant. For example, if the return value is equal to vbOK constant then the user will have pressed the OK button. Note that the following VB constants may be used:

Table 13.1. The MsgBox() function's return value constants and their values.

Constant	Value
vbOK	1
vbCancel	2
vbAbort	3
vbRetry	4
vbIgnore	5
vbYes	6
vbNo	7

Listing 13.1 Using the MsgBox() function's return value.

Dim msgBoxValue as Integer

msgBoxValue = MsgBox ("Invalid Password. Try again?", _

vbError+vbRetryCancel

If msgBoxValue = vbRetry then

'Call LoginProcedure again

Else

End

End if

In Listing 13.1, we have given an example of how to use the MsgBox function's return value to identify which button was pressed. Here's a short interpretation of this code. We have configured the message box to display the error icon and two buttons: Retry and Cancel. This means that we may expect the message box to return two possible values: vbCancel or vbRetry. Thus, we check if the return value is equal to vbRetry. If it is, we continue the login process. If not, we shut down the application. Note that this code is used in Project 11 to respond to an invalid user ID or password in the login procedure.

4. How to Compile an Application

To finalize the process of application development, you need to compile the application. When an application is compiled, the VB compiler program will translate the programming code that you have written into binary machine instructions. As a result of this work, an executable file with the ".exe" file name extension will be created. You can run the executable file on any windows machine as long as all system and VB runtime dependencies and all application specific dependencies are installed on that machine. We will talk about application dependencies in Lesson 14.

To compile the application you need to do the following:

Step 1: On the File menu, choose Make LoginProject.exe. This will bring up the Make Project dialog box.

Step 2: In the Make Project dialog box, navigate to the folder where you would like to store the executable file.

Step 3: In the File Name text box, type the desired executable file name and click on the OK button.

Test the executable file.

Once you have successfully compiled the application, it might be a good idea to test the executable file. To test the executable file, do the following:

- In Windows Explorer, locate the executable file.
- To start the program double-click the executable file.

If the executable works properly and provides all the expected functionality, you have successfully completed the application development process.

Homework Assignment Project

Introduction

This project is going to be very exciting and will bring you very close to real world enterprise projects. In this project, you will use the Sub Main as a startup object and write code in a standard module that will be used as a dispatcher that controls the execution process. The login form will be used in conjunction with the Sub Main to authenticate the user and decide whether to allow or deny access to the application. Finally, you will compile your application to make an executable file.

1. Create and Save Project 11: LoginProject

1.   In Windows Explorer create a new folder and name it *Project11.*

2.   In Windows Explorer copy five objects from Project10 to Project11 folder. These objects should include: frmMenus, frmData, cCamcorder, cCamera and cConnect.

3.   Copy Inventory.mdb Access database file to Project11 folder.

4.   Open the VB IDE and create a New Standard EXE project.

5.   Set the project name to "LoginProject".

6.   Add all five objects to the new project. On the Project menu choose Add Form; select Existing; Navigate to Project11 folder and select frmMenus; click Open. Repeat this operation with the frmData form. Add three class modules: cCamcorder,

cCamera and cConnect objects. Make sure that you first copy these objects from Project10 to Project11 folder and then add them to the project.

7.   Rename the Form1 form as frmLogin.

8.   Save the frmLogin form to Project11 folder.

9.   Add a standard module. On the Project menu, choose Add Module; click on the New tab; select Module and click on the Open button. In Project Explorer, highlight the module, click on the Properties button, and change the name property to AppModule. Save the new module in Project11 folder.

10.   On the File menu, choose Save Project As; navigate to the project folder and save the project file in it.

11.   Add a new table to your Access database file. From MS Access open your Inventory.mdb file and add a new table. In this table create two columns: UserID and Password as text. Save the table as Users. Open

the table in the Open mode and enter two users:
James Bond with the password 007 and Mary
Blond with the password 008.

Reference the ADO Library. On the Project menu, choose
References and check Microsoft ActiveX Data Objects 2.5 Library;
then click OK. If you do not have ADO version 2.5, select the latest
version.

2. Add Controls and Set their Properties

Set frmLogin form objects properties according to Table 13.2.

Table 13.2. The frmLogin Form Object Properties.

Object	Property	Setting
Form	name	frmLogin
Label	caption	User ID:
Label2	caption	Password:
CommandButton	name	cmdOK
	Caption:	&OK
CommandButton	name	cmdCancel
	Caption	&Cancel

Your competed frmLogin form should look like the one shown in Figure 13.1. When you have added all the objects to your project, you should be able to see seven modules in your Project Explorer. In Figure 13.5, you can see the Project Explorer that shows the LoginProject project modules.

Figure 13.5. The Project Explorer.

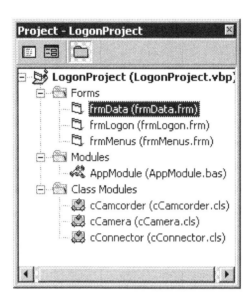

3. Write the Application Code

In this application, you will use seven modules: three form modules, three class modules, and one standard module. You will write code only in the standard module and in the frmLogin form.

a) Write the Sub Main procedure

In this project, you will write code to authenticate the user. You will write the Sub Main procedure in the AppModule standard module. Your Sub Main code should look like this:

```
Public Sub Main()
Dim blnResponse As Boolean
If frmLogin.fLogOn = True Then
frmMenus.Show 1
End If
End Sub
```

b) Write code in the frmLogin form

1. Declare a module level variable in the General section:

```
Option Explicit
```

Private UserOK As Boolean

2. Write this code in the form load event:

Private Sub Form_Load()

Me.Top = (Screen.Height - Me.Height) / 2

Me.Left = (Screen.Width - Me.Width) / 2

End Sub

3. Write the fLogin function.

The fLogin function is declared public because it is meant to be visible from other modules in the application. This function is very important because it fulfills a number of tasks in the application. First, it is used as a gateway to the frmLogin form. Then it shows the frmLogin from and checks the value of the UserOK variable that we created to monitor the user authentication process and the user's decision to cancel the login process.

In the user authentication process, we have several options: for example, we may decide to allow the user to enter User ID and Password an unlimited number of times, or we may limit the number of attempts. We have chosen to implement an unlimited number of attempts version. You will be given an extra credit task to implement a limited version..

Pay attention to how we manage the execution of code in the frmLogin form. We use the form's *Show* method to display the form in modal form and then we call the *Unload* form method when we know that the authentication is complete or when the user clicks Cancel. In all other situations, we use the *Exit* function statement to stay in the same mode and keep the form displayed.

Public Function fLogin() As Boolean

fLogin = False

frmLogin.Show 1

If UserOK = True Then

fLogin = True

Souleiman Valiev

> *Unload Me*

End If

End Function

4. Write the ValidateInput function. This function should check if txtUserID and txtPWD text boxes are filled with data. We call this procedure when the user clicks on the OK button.

Private Function ValidateInput() As Boolean

ValidateInput = False

If txtUserID <> "" Then

If txtPwd <> "" Then

ValidateInput = True

Else

MsgBox "Enter Password."

txtPwd.SetFocus

Exit Function

End If

Else

MsgBox "Enter User ID."

txtUserID.SetFocus

Exit Function

End If

End Function

5. Write the CheckUserID function.

This function does the verification work. It queries the Users table to find out if such a user exists and if the provided password is identical to the one retrieved from the database. If the user forgets to type in the user ID or password, he is prompted to do so. If an invalid user ID or password is entered, an error message is displayed. Finally, if the user clicks on the Cancel button, it shuts down the application. Note that we use the MsgBox() function, the Unload form method and the Exit Function statement to manage this communication with the user.

Private Function CheckUserID() As Integer

511

Souleiman Valiev

```
Dim errorMsg As String

Dim strUserID As String

Dim strPwd As String

Dim cDBCon As cConnector

Dim sql As String

Dim rs As ADODB.Recordset

Dim iRetVal As Integer

CheckUserID = 0 'false

strUserID = txtUserID

strPwd = txtPwd

sql = "Select password from Users where"

sql = sql & "UserID Like" & "'" & strUserID & "'"

Set cDBCon = New cConnector

If Not cDBCon.GetData(sql, rs) Then

errorMsg = "Connection failed. Try again?"

iRetVal = MsgBox(errorMsg, vbCritical + vbRetryCancel)

If iRetVal = vbCancel Then

UserOK = False

Unload Me
```

Else

Exit Function

End If

End If

If rs.BOF Or rs.EOF Then

errorMsg = "Invalid User ID. Try again?"

iRetVal = MsgBox(errorMsg, vbCritical + vbRetryCancel)

If iRetVal = vbCancel Then

UserOK = False

Unload Me

Else

Exit Function

End If

End If

If strPwd = rs("Password") Then

CheckUserID = True

Exit Function

Else

errorMsg = "Invalid Password. Try again?"

iRetVal = MsgBox(errorMsg, vbCritical + vbRetryCancel)

If iRetVal = vbCancel Then

UserOK = False

Unload Me

Else

Exit Function

End If

End If

End Function

6. Call the ValidateInput and the CheckUserID procedures from the cmdOK click event procedure:

Private Sub cmdOK_Click()

If ValidateInput = True Then

If CheckUserID = True Then

UserOK = True

Unload Me

End If

End If

End Sub

5. Call the *Unload* method from the cmdCancel click event procedure:

Private Sub cmdCancel_Click()

   UserOK = False

   Unload Me

End Sub

4. Run and Test the Application

After you have debugged your application and fixed errors, do the following testing.

1. Start the application and enter User ID: James; Password: 007. Does the application open the Menus form?

2.   Start the application and in the login form click OK without any data entered. Do you get a prompt: Enter UserID.

3.   Enter any user ID but no password. Do you get a prompt: Enter Password?

4.   Enter James as the user ID and any password. Do you get an error message: Invalid password. Try again?

5.   Enter any User ID and any Password. Do you get the message: Invalid UserID. Try Again?

6.   Test the Application in any possible way and see if you can find any bugs.

Congratulations! You have completed your application testing.

5. Compile your Application

With the project open in the VB IDE, go to the File menu and choose Make LoginProject.exe. This task is relatively simple but it should be done only after you have thoroughly debugged and tested your application. Remember, when you try to compile the application, the compiler will check the syntax and variable declaration and some other errors. If any error is found, the compilation will stop and an error message will be displayed. You should fix the error and try to compile again. Once the compilation has gone through OK, you should test the executable file created by the compiler. Make sure that you know where you saved the executable file. Double-click the executable file and the application will start. Do as much testing of the executable as possible and only then proceed to creating a Setup program.

6. Extra Credit Tasks

1.   There is one nasty bug that wakes up when you login with a wrong User ID and Password and click on the OK and then on the Cancel button. Try to detect and fix this bug.

2.	The current version of your applications allows unlimited attempts to login with wrong user ID or password. Redesign the application to allow only two login attempts. Hint: you need to alter your code in the frmLogin form by creating a static or module level variable that will store the number of login attempts and check that number whenever the user authentication is performed. If the number exceeds two, the application must be shut down.

3.	Write the error handler code in CheckUserID procedure.

Congratulations! You have successfully completed Lesson 13.

Lesson 14

Lesson 14

How to Create a Setup Program

In this Lesson:

You will create Project 11; you will learn how to create a Setup program for your VB application. You will use the VB Package and Deployment Wizard to create an installation program.

Contents of Lesson 14

Part A: Create Your Homework Project

1. Create Project 11

2. Project 11 Bug Description

3. Project 11 Bug Fix

4. Project 11 Extra Credit Task

Part B: How to Create an Installation Program

1. What is a Setup Program?

2. How a Program is Installed?

a) Granting a Permanent Resident Status

b) Copying Files and Registering Components

4. How to Create an Installation Program

5. How to Uninstall a Program

Part C: Homework Assignment Project

1. Create *Project12* Folder

2. Compile the Application

3. Create the Application Setup Program

4. Run the Setup Program on your Computer

5. Run and Test the Installed Program

Create Your Homework Project

1. Create Project 11

Create Project 11 according to the homework assignment described in Lesson 13. It is very important to complete this project before continuing with this lesson.

2. Project 11 Bug Description

To see this bug, do the following: run the application; in the login form enter any invalid user ID and password; and click OK. You should get the error message: "Invalid UserID. Try again?" If you click Retry, the application will show you a login form again, but if you click Cancel you should get the "BOF or EOF unhanded error" error message.

The bug that we are looking for lives in the CkheckUserID function that is shown in Listing 14.1. Place a breakpoint at the beginning of the CheckUserID procedure and attempt to login as described above. You should see that after the MsgBox() function return value is checked, the execution of code in that procedure continues and hits the place where it tries to read the "password" field of the recordset. The problem is that the recordset is empty and the end of file property (EOF) is true. The recordset is empty because we have not populated it with the necessary data yet. To solve this problem we must make sure that when the user clicks Cancel this part of code is not executed.

3. Project 11 Bug Fix

This bug fix is simple. We should exit the function, even though we call the Unload form method. And since we should exit the function no matter what button is clicked by the user we can write

Exit Function one time before the last *End If* statement. Your redesigned code of this function should look like Listing 14.1.

Listing 14.1 The CheckUserID Procedure after bug fix.

Private Function CheckUserID() As Integer

Dim errorMsg As String

Dim ErrDes As String

Dim ErrNum As Long

Dim strUserID As String

Dim strPwd As String

Dim cDBCon As cConnector

Dim sql As String

Dim rs As ADODB.Recordset

Dim iRetVal As Integer

On Error GoTo UserIDErr

'Default to False

CheckUserID = 0

strUserID = txtUserID

Souleiman Valiev

strPwd = txtPwd

sql = "Select password from Users where UserID Like "

sql =sql & """ & strUserID & """

Set cDBCon = New cConnector

If Not cDBCon.GetData(sql, rs) Then

errorMsg = "Connection failed. Try again?"

iRetVal = MsgBox(errorMsg, vbCritical + vbRetryCancel)

If iRetVal = vbCancel Then

UserOK = False

Unload Me

Else

Exit Function

End If

End If

If rs.BOF Or rs.EOF Then

errorMsg = "Invalid User ID. Try again?"

iRetVal = MsgBox(errorMsg, vbCritical + vbRetryCancel)

If iRetVal = vbCancel Then

'Tthe bug is here

```
UserOK = False

Unload Me

Exit Function

Else

        Exit Function

End If

End If

If strPwd = rs("Password") Then

CheckUserID = True

Exit Function

Else

errorMsg = "Invalid Password. Try again?"

iRetVal = MsgBox(errorMsg, vbCritical + vbRetryCancel)

If iRetVal = vbCancel Then

UserOK = False

Unload Me

Else

Exit Function

End If
```

Souleiman Valiev

End If

Exit Function

UserIDErr:

ErrNum = Err.Number

ErrDes = Err.Description

Err.Raise ErrNum, "Check UserID", ErrDes

End Function

4. Project 11 Extra Credit Task

To get an extra credit, write code that will keep track of how many times the user tried to login. Your task is to alter the CheckUserID procedure in such a way that it will allow only two login attempts. After two attempts to login with the wrong userID or Password, the application must shut down without any notification. To implement this logic do the following:

Step 1: Declare a module level variable in the General section.

Dim LoginAttempts As Integer

Step 2: At the very beginning of the CheckUserID procedure, check the value of the LoginAttempts variable. If it is greater than 2 shut down the application. Your code may look like this:

If LoginAttempts > 2 Then

    UserOK = False

    End

End If

Step 3: Increment the value of the LoginAttempts variable.

Note that you need to increment the value of the LoginAttempts variable each time the CheckUserID procedure is executed. Note that the LoginAttempts variable is declared a module level variable so that it can hold the value between the CheckUserID procedure calls. The following line of code will increment the LoginAttempts variable's value:

Souleiman Valiev

LoginAttempts = LoginAttempts + 1

.

532

How to Create an Installation Program

1. What is a Setup Program?

Why do we need a setup program? The setup program does a lot of hard work that may require expert knowledge and experience to do manually. In short, a setup program is like a skilled technician who knows how to copy and permanently install system and application specific files on a target computer. To understand how that hypothetical technician does it, let's take a closer look at the work that should be done to install a program

2. How a Program is Installed?

a) Granting a Permanent Resident Status

Figuratively speaking, the installation of a program can be compared with granting a program a permanent residency status. Thus, when we decide to grant this status to a certain program on a certain computer, the program must be moved to that computer. When the program moves, it wants its entire vital environment to be moved there as well. So, a permanent resident must be moved with all its baggage, luggage, love seats and beloved pets. A program will not function properly if not all these requisites are hanging around. For example, a Visual Basic application will not run without a VB runtime DLL and some windows system files. In addition, the application won't function properly without application specific components and some data or report files. To cut a long story short, all these requisites must be copied and properly installed on the target machine.

b) Copying Files and Registering Components

The main task of a setup program is to copy and install all the necessary files and components on the target computer. The application is normally represented by one exe file and a set of dependency files. Application dependency files may be divided into the following categories:

- System files

- VB runtime system files

- Application specific components

- Application specific data files.

It is important to understand that it is necessary not just to copy these files to the target computer but also to register all components properly.

When you need to install a program?

If you want to run your program on the computer where you developed it using MS Visual Studio, you actually do not need to install it. All you need to do is create an executable file by compiling the project and then you are free to move that file to any directory and run it. You may also create a shortcut to the program executable file and then run the program by double-clicking the shortcut. However, what if you want to let other users install and use your program on their own machines. In this case, you need to consider all the requirements mentioned above and use a setup program to install your program.

3. How does a Setup Program Work?

A detailed description of a setup program's work is definitely outside this book's scope. Here's a very brief description of how a setup program does the installation work. In the first phase, the setup copies all installation files from the installation media or directory to a temporary directory on the target computer. In the second phase, the setup creates an application directory; copies application specific files into that directory; copies all system and application specific files to their appropriate directories; registers all components; and creates the program's menu group in the Programs menu. The setup is smart enough to know which file to put in which directory and how components should be registered. As a result, the setup actually automates the whole process of installing a program on any computer.

4. How to Create an Installation Program

Creating a setup program is normally done when you have finished application development and testing. To start creating the installation program, you should have the project and the program executable files ready. The VB Package and Deployment Wizard automate the process and are relatively simple to use. Please find systematic instructions for creating a setup program in your homework assignment for Project 12.

5. How to Uninstall a Program

Uninstalling a program is a very responsible process because any improper removal of a program may cause serious problems for other applications on the same machine. A typical uninstall process does the following work: it deletes all application specific files from the application directory, and it unregisters application specific and some shared components. There are at least two legal ways of uninstalling a program from a computer. You may use the Uninstall menu if it was created in the application menu group in the Programs menu. Or you can use the Add/Remove programs utility, which you can find in the Control Panel. Remember any manual removal of application specific or application related files may create potentially serious problems for other applications. In addition, removing application files from the application directory before uninstall may make it difficult to uninstall that program properly. A program should be removed only using one of the uninstall methods. After you have successfully uninstalled the application, you need to manually delete

the application folder.

Homework Assignment Project

Introduction

This project is different from all our previous projects. You are not going to create another application. You need to create a program that will handle the installation of your program on any computer. A program that installs an application on a user's machine is called a Setup program. Such programs may be created using the VB Package and the Deployment Wizard. Before you start creating a Setup program you should have the following two files ready:

- The application executable file with the file name extension "exe".

541

- The project file with the file name extension "vbp".

It is very important to make sure that all project dependencies are properly installed on your computer. Remember that an application may have such dependencies as COM DLLs, data files, report files, system files and so on. If you get an error message "Missing dependencies" when creating a setup program, you should stop the process, install the missing files and then continue. Remember, choosing to ignore the "Missing dependencies" message may cause problems in the installed application.

1. Create *Project12* Folder

In Windows Explorer, create Project12 folder.

2. Compile the Application

If you did not compile the application in Project 11, you need to return to Project 11 and complete it.

3. Create the Application Setup Program

We will break this process into consecutive steps.

Step 1: Start the Package and Deployment Wizard

On the Programs menu, choose Microsoft Visual Studio 6.0; then choose Microsoft Visual Studio 6.0 Tools, and then choose Package & Deployment Wizard. This should bring up the dialog box shown in Figure 14.1.

Figure 14.1 The Package and Deployment Wizard.

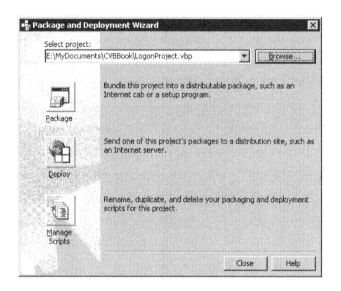

Step 2: Specify the project file

In the Package and Deployment Wizard dialog box, click on the Browse button and navigate to the folder where your project files are located. In our case, it should be Project11 folder. Select the project file with the file name extension "vbp". Again, in our case, it should be the LoginProject.vbp file. When you have completed navigation to the project file, you should return to the Package and

Deployment Wizard dialog box. Now check if the project file path and name are displayed correctly in the Project File drop down list box.

Step 3: Click on the Package button

The installation package creation process will start. If you have made any changes to the project files after compiling the project, the Package and Deployment Wizard will inform you about it and will offer you the option of recompiling the project. Click No if you want to disregard the changes. This should bring up the Package Type dialog box shown in Figure 14.2.

Figure 14.2. Package Type dialog box.

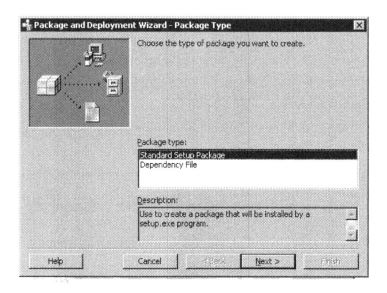

Step 4: Select the Package Type

In the Package Type dialog box select Standard Setup Package and click Next. This will bring up the Package Folder dialog box shown in Figure 14.3.

Figure 14.3. The Package Folder dialog box.

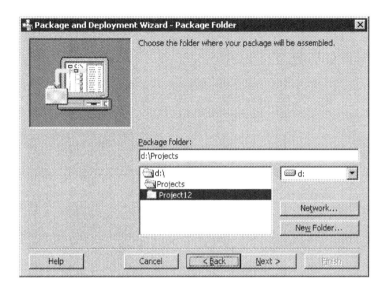

Step 5. Select the folder or type the path

At this point, you should decide where you want to create your setup package. In fact, you have created Project12 folder to store the setup package. So, navigate to it and check if the path is correctly shown in the "Package folder:" text box. By default, the Package and Deployment Wizard will suggest you create a "Package" folder in your suggested directory. To accept, click Next. Because the Package

547

folder does not exist in your project folder, you will receive a message suggesting you create it. Click Yes. In the next screen, you may see a Missing Dependency Information window that complains about missing components information that your application might be using. One such component may be the ADO component, which may be listed as MSADO25.tlb. If you do receive this message, you may want to close the Package and Deployment Wizard and do the following: go back to your project, and in the References dialog box check the latest version of ADO in your system. You may have ADO 2.7 and some earlier versions (2.5, 2.1). Then use any search utility to verify if you have the MDAC_TYP.exe file in your system. If you do not have it, copy it from the Microsoft Visual Studio 6.0 disk 1 or download it from the MSDN site. Then recompile your project and start the Package and Deployment Wizard again. If you have not stopped the process, click on the Next button and you should see the Included Files dialog box shown in Figure 14.4.

Figure 14.4 The Included Files dialog box.

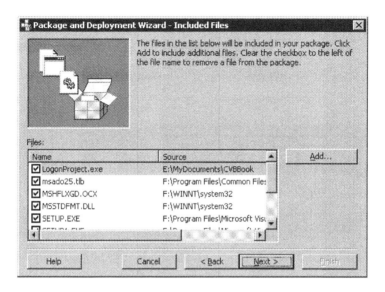

Step 6: In the Included Files dialog box

In the Included Files dialog box, check if the application executable file and all project dependency files are listed. For instance, the first two files should be the LoginProject.exe and the MDAC_TYP.exe. The Package and Deployment Wizard is smart enough to list all dependencies if they are present on your machine.

Click on the Next button. This should bring up the Cab Options dialog

box shown in Figure 14.5.

Figure 14.5 The Cab Options dialog box.

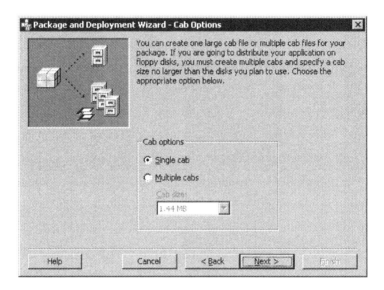

Step 7: Cab Options Dialog Box

In this window, you may choose a Single Cab or Multiple

Cabs. Choosing a single cab means that one package will be created

with all Setup and Support files in it. If you choose multiple cabs, you will have to specify the size of each cab. Select Single Cab and click

on the Next button. This should bring up the Installation Title dialog

box shown in Figure 14.6.

Figure 14.6. The Installation Title dialog box.

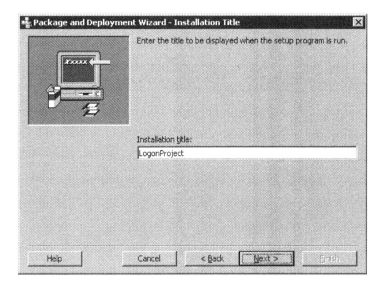

Step 8. The Installation Title Dialog Box

In the Installation Title dialog box, you are given the chance to

set the title of your program's installation screen. The Package and

Deployment Wizard will suggest your project name but you may change it to something else. For example, type in this: Login Project Setup Program. Now click Next. This will bring up the Start Menu Items dialog box shown in Figure 14.7.

Figure 14.7 The Start Menu Items dialog box.

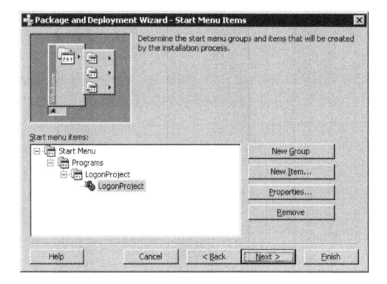

Step 9. The Start Menu Items Dialog Box.

In the Start Menu Items dialog box, you can type in the name of each item related to your program. You may want to have a group of items that include the program name, the help menu name and the uninstall menus. In fact, this window shows how the application title will look in the Programs menu. Accept the default and click on the Next button. This will bring up the Install Locations dialog box shown in Figure 14.8.

Figure 14.8. The Install Locations dialog box.

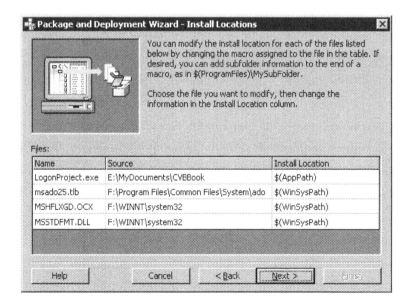

Step 10: The Install Locations Dialog Box

This window will show you the folders where the Setup Program will copy system and application specific files. The installation files should be installed into several types of directories. For example, the system files should be stored in the System/System32 directory and the application specific files should be copied to the application directory. To change the target location of files requires advanced knowledge and experience. So, accept the defaults and click on the Next button. This will bring up the Shared Files dialog box shown in Figure 14.9.

Figure 14.9. The Shared Files dialog box.

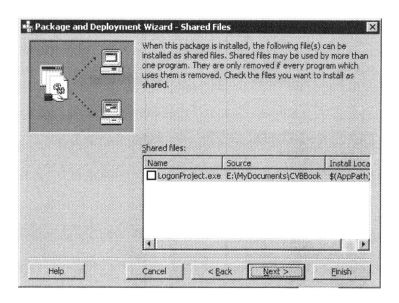

Step 11. The Shared Files Dialog Box

This window should show all shared files. Note that shared files may be used by other programs in your computer. It is very unlikely that other programs will use your Login Project program, so you should not check it as shared. However, you may check MDAC_TYP.exe because there may be programs that use it. Click on the Next button. This should bring up the Finished window shown in Figure 14.10.

Figure 14.10. The Finished dialog box.

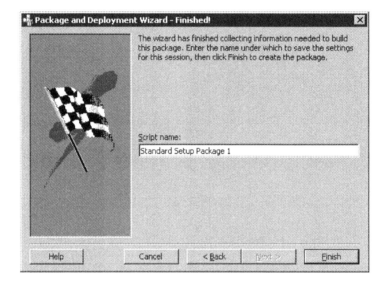

Step 12: The Finished Dialog Box

This window will show the Setup script file name. You can change it or accept the default. The setup script is stored in a designated folder and can be used to modify the Setup program in the future. Click on the Finish button. This will bring up the Packaging

Report dialog box shown in Figure 14.11.

Figure 14.11 The Packaging Report dialog box.

Step 13: The Packaging Report Dialog Box

The Packaging Report shown in Figure 14.11 carries two

pieces of important information: it shows the directory where your application setup package cab file has been built; and it informs you that the batch file was created in the support directory. You may save the report or ignore it and click Close.

Congratulations! You have successfully created a setup program.

4. Run the Setup Program on your Computer

If you have successfully created your setup program, you can now test it on your computer. To test your setup program do the following:

1.   In Windows Explorer, locate the folder where you created a Setup Package.

2.   There should be four items in your Package folder: Support folder, LoginProject.cab file, Setup.exe, and Setup.lst.

3.   To start the Setup program, double-click the Setup.exe file.

4.   To complete the installation, follow the Setup program's instructions.

5. Run and Test the Installed Program

If you managed to successfully install your program on your computer, it is time to give it a good test. To test your newly installed program, do the following:

1. On the Programs menu, choose Login Project.

2. Test your application.

Congratulations! You have successfully completed Lesson 14, and this course. Good luck!

Bibliography

Microsoft Corporation. *Microsoft Visual Basic 6.0 Programmer's Guide.* Microsoft Press,

1998. (ISBN 1-57231-863-5)

John Clark Craig, Jeff Webb. *Microsoft Visual Basic 6.0 Developer's Workshop.* Microsoft Press, 1998. (ISBN 1-57231-883-X)

Evangelos Petroutsos. *Mastering Visual Basic 6.* SYBEX. 1998. (ISBN 0-7821-2272-8)

Dale Rogerson. Inside COM. Microsoft's Component Object Model. Microsoft Press. 1997. (ISBN 1-57231-349-8)

About the Author

Souleiman Valiev holds a Ph.D. in Applied Linguistics from Saint Petersburg Institute of Linguistics, Russian Academy of Sciences. His professional interests lie in the field of computer speech technology, including speech synthesis and recognition. His background includes working as a senior software engineer and as a consultant for companies, and the design of client server and distributed Internet applications. Please send comments or questions to anvarius@hotmail.com

www.ingramcontent.com/pod-product-compliance
Lightning Source LLC
Chambersburg PA
CBHW051219050326
40689CB00007B/734